A Practical Guide to

First published 1997
© Royal College of Obstetricians and Gynaecologists 1997
ISBN 0-902331-93-0

Published by the **RCOG Press** at the
Royal College of Obstetricians and Gynaecologists
27 Sussex Place, Regent's Park
London NW1 4RG
Registered Charity No. 213280

Designed by Geoffrey Wadsley
Printed by Latimer Trend & Company Ltd, Plymouth

Contents

CONTENTS

Preface

The purpose of this book is to provide basic guidelines for those starting their training in gynaecology. It will also provide continuing help for trainees in the early part of their training and hopefully others working in gynaecology and general practice.

The guidelines detailed in this particular volume are not intended to replace those that may already be in place in any particular unit. Practice varies considerably by virtue of local resource and the needs of individual units and patient populations. Nevertheless, many trainees have expressed the opinion that the differences between gynaecology and other disciplines is sufficient, at least when starting out, to warrant some form of basic guidance. Most practitioners at this stage of their careers are aware that there is usually more than one way to manage most problems and, again, this text does not set out to be didactic. You should always endeavour to discuss investigation and management with those responsible for your training. Texts such as these are meant to help with training; they are not a substitute for clinical training in the clinic, ward and theatre.

Acknowledgements

We would like to thank our colleagues for their help and suggestions and also the trainees at the City Hospital NHS Trust, Dudley Road, Birmingham for their comments and contributions. We would also wish to thank all those District Tutors of the Royal College of Obstetricians and Gynaecologists who provided copies of guidelines that they already use in their clinical practices. This text, we hope, represents a distillate of many opinions and attitudes.

David Luesley   March 1997
John Watts

Commonly used abbreviations in gynaecology

AID   Artificial insemination using donor semen, as opposed to
            AIH which is artificial insemination using husband's or
            partner's semen. The latter is usually specially prepared and
            injected high into the uterine cavity (high intrauterine
            insemination – HIUI)

AIS   Adenocarcinoma-in-situ. A glandular pre-invasive condi-
            tion of the cervix, less common than its squamous counter-
            part, CIN (see below)

BSO   Bilateral salpingo-oophorectomy. A surgical procedure
            removing both ovaries and fallopian tubes

BTB   Breakthrough bleeding. A term usually applied to the
            bleeding occasionally noticed by some women using
            combined oral contraception. The bleeding occurs whilst
            the pill is being taken and not in the pill-free week. Bleeding
            in the pill-free week is normal and is termed withdrawal
            bleeding

CIN   Cervical intraepithelial neoplasia. A premalignant condi-
            tion of the cervix

COC   Combined oral contraceptive. This refers to steroid oral
            contraceptives containing an oestrogen, usually ethinyl-
            oestradiol, and a progestogen

D&C   Dilatation and curettage. An operative procedure, usually
            performed under a general anaesthetic. The cervix is dilated
            using a graduated set of dilators to a level where a curette
            can be introduced into the uterine cavity. This is then used
            to scrape endometrial or other tissue from the endometrium
            for histological analysis. The procedure is diagnostic. It is
            not a treatment for menstrual dysfunction

DUB   Dysfunctional uterine bleeding. Excessive (>80 ml) or
            erratic menstruation where no recognisable pathology can

be found. Pathologies to exclude that might account for menorrhagia or irregular cycles include fibroids, endometriosis, pelvic inflammatory disease or endometrial hyperplasia or neoplasia

ERPOC Evacuation of retained products of conception. Also referred to as an 'Evac.'. This is an operative procedure performed under general, regional or local anaesthetic whereby residual placental and fetal tissue are scraped off the uterine walls following an incomplete abortion

FIGO International Federation of Obstetrics and Gynecology. An international body that provides standards for classification such as staging procedures for gynaecological malignancies

FSH Follicle-stimulating hormone

GIFT Gamete intrafallopian transfer. A method of assisted conception. Ova and sperm are inserted into the distal end of the fallopian tube under laparoscopic guidance to allow fertilisation to occur in the ampullary portion of the tube

GUM Genitourinary medicine

HPV Human papillomavirus. A group of DNA viruses. Many subtypes have been identified, some of which may be onco-genic. Of particular interest in pre-invasive and invasive disease of the cervix where they may be implicated in the neoplastic process (esp. Types 16 and 18)

HRT Hormone replacement therapy. Replacement of oestrogen alone or with progestogen in naturally menopausal women or in women who have had their ovaries removed. HRT is also given in situations of absent or low oestrogen production such as Turner's syndrome. In cases where the uterus remains *in situ*, i.e. not hysterectomised, a progestogen should also be given to minimise the risk of hyperplasia and neoplasia

HSG Hysterosalpingogram. An imaging technique whereby radio-opaque dye is infused through a specially designed applicator through the endocervical canal. Its purpose is to highlight the endometrial cavity for abnormalities of shape and contour and also to outline the fallopian tubes. This will determine any blockage, the level and to some extent the nature of the blockage. It is usually performed as an adjunct to fertility investigations especially prior to planned tubal surgery

HSV   Herpes simplex virus. Two subtypes: Type I and Type II. Both may cause genital herpes

IMB   Intermenstrual bleeding. Any vaginal bleeding occurring between what a woman regards as normal menses. This may be midcycle as can occur at ovulation (although usually quite light) or pre-menstrual spotting

IUCD   Intrauterine contraceptive device. Often referred to by women as a coil. This is a plastic device, usually containing a copper component, that is inserted into the uterine cavity as a form of contraception

IVF   *In vitro* fertilisation. Ova are collected from either natural or more usually stimulated cycles under ultrasound guidance. The collected ova are then mixed with sperm and fertilisation and early embryogenesis are supported in artificial media outside the body. The early embryo is transferred back to the endometrial cavity by the transcervical route. This was the first type of popularised assisted conception and is appropriate for women with either non-functional or absent fallopian tubes where GIFT and ZIFT would be inappropriate

K   Koilocytosis. A short term used to describe the cytological and histological features associated with human papillomavirus infection (see HPV)

Lap+Dye Laparoscopy and tubal patency test. An endoscopic procedure using a laparoscope to visualise the pelvic organs and by injecting a coloured dye into the endometrial cavity via the cervix, the patency of the fallopian tubes can be assessed. Also referred to as TPT (tubal patency test)

LH   Luteinising hormone

LLETZ   Large loop excision of the transformation zone. A diathermy excision technique for the treatment of women with cervical intraepithelial neoplasia

LMP   Last menstrual period. This refers to the first day of the woman's last period; that is, the day that menstruation began. An average cycle lasts 28 days of which 3–7 days will be days of menstruation. The least consistent part of the cycle is the follicular phase, whereas the luteal phase usually lasts about 14 days. Ovulation therefore occurs about 14 days prior to menstruation

COMMONLY USED ABBREVIATIONS IN GYNAECOLOGY

OCP   Oral contraceptive pill. This is a generic term for both combined (COC) and progestogen-only (POP) pills

PCB   Postcoital bleeding. Vaginal bleeding occurring either during or after penetrative intercourse. Whilst carcinoma of the cervix may cause this, so can benign conditions such as a cervical ectropion. Some bleeding is not unusual following the first time a woman has intercourse

PCO   Polycystic ovary

PCT   Postcoital test. Examination of a sample of cervical mucus shortly after sexual intercourse. This is done to assess the number and forward motility of sperms. It also shows if intercourse has taken place properly

PID   Pelvic inflammatory disease. Refers to infection of the uterine tubes or ovaries. Most likely pathogens are gonococci, chlamydia or anaerobes

PMB   Postmenopausal bleeding. This describes any episode of vaginal bleeding occurring after the menopause. The latter is usually defined as a period of 12 months' amenorrhoea which may or may not be associated with other climacteric symptoms such as hot flushes, vaginal dryness, etc.

PMS/PMT Pre-menstrual syndrome or pre-menstrual tension. A cyclical disorder seen classically in the week prior to normal menstruation. Characterised by both physical (bloating, breast tenderness, oedema) and emotional (mood swings, irritability, depression and tearfulness) symptoms

POD   Pouch of Douglas. A peritoneum-lined space lying between the posterior aspect of the cervix and upper vagina and the anterior aspect of the rectum. If this prolapses down into the vagina an enterocoele forms. May contain loops of small bowel

POP   Progestogen-only pill. Oral contraceptive pill containing only progestogen

RaFEA   Radiofrequency endometrial ablation. A means of destroying the endometrium yet leaving the uterus intact. This technique employs a microwave principle to generate heat in the endometrium and therefore lead to its permanent destruction. It is used to treat dysfunctional uterine bleeding

STD   Sexually transmitted disease. An infection contracted by sexual contact

TAH   Total abdominal hysterectomy. A surgical procedure to remove the uterus and cervix

TCRE   Transcervical resection of the endometrium. A technique where the endometrium is resected hysteroscopically using a fine diathermy loop. This is a treatment for menorrhagia that conserves the uterus

TZ   Transformation zone. An area on the cervix between squamous epithelium and glandular epithelium where dysplasia and metaplasia occur

Vag. Hyst.   Vaginal hysterectomy. A surgical procedure to remove the uterus and cervix when the approach is through the vagina. Usually combined with a repair procedure at the same time

VE/PV   Vaginal examination (PV – *per vaginam*). A standard part of the basic gynaecological examination. The procedure is often called a **bimanual** examination as the fingers of one examining hand are placed in the vagina whilst the other hand is used to palpate the lower abdomen

ZIFT   Zygote intrafallopian transfer. Similar to GIFT but fertilisation and thus zygote formation occurs outside the body. The zygote is transferred back to the distal end of the fallopian tube to allow the early part of embryogenesis to occur in its natural environment

1 *General principles*

Gynaecology is a very sensitive specialty with many areas touching on aspects of the lives of women and their families that is not frequently seen in other branches of acute medicine. It is therefore of vital importance that the primary assessment is both accurate and conducted in a manner that is minimally intrusive and preserves the woman's dignity.

As many gynaecological problems are both physically distressing and a source of anxiety for women, it is not surprising that there is often a 'hidden agenda'. In these situations, finding out what the major problem actually is can be a lengthy and difficult process. Patience, empathy and above all confidentiality are therefore important if one is to achieve the desired objective.

THE GYNAECOLOGICAL HISTORY

History taking is a clinical skill and cannot be done purely by having a checklist of standard questions. However, it might be valuable initially to adopt a semistructured approach to such interviews. Having said this, it is important that some basic areas are covered (in addition to the presenting complaint), as they are of greater importance in gynaecology than in other areas. Table 1.1 shows the areas that should always be included at the initial interview.

Sometimes it is not possible to obtain the ideal history. Patients who are severely ill, collapsed or mentally infirm are such examples. It is important in these situations to try and get as much information as possible from either a relative or friend and note the source of the information.

Table 1.1 Areas to be covered at the initial interview	
Menstrual history	LMP.* Age of menarche, menopause, cycle frequency, duration of bleeding, associated pain, etc.
Past obstetric history	Number of children, last childbirth, complications, if any. Number of miscarriages (and weeks gestation at which they occurred). Therapeutic terminations (and weeks gestation at which they occurred). Complications following terminations or miscarriages
Previous gynaecological problems	Ongoing treatment, e.g. infertility
Previous pelvic surgery	
Fertility status	i.e. future reproductive plans
Current and past contraception	Method(s), duration, side-effects
Other episodes of vaginal bleeding	Postcoital bleeding, intermenstrual bleeding, postmenopausal bleeding
Any problems with bowel or bladder function	
Cervical smear history	Last smear, when and result; any previous treatment for abnormal smears?
Current relationship	i.e. new partner
Social factors	Smoking, alcohol, employment
Family history	Inherited disorders, malignancies, e.g. ovary, breast or bowel
Sexual activity or problems	

* **LMP**: The date of the last menstrual period (when it started) is very important. **All women within the reproductive age range could be pregnant**. This should be considered in all situations.

THE GYNAECOLOGICAL EXAMINATION

The woman should be put at ease and the nature of the examination explained to her prior to starting. Privacy is essential and it is equally essential that a chaperone is present for male doctors. This is for both the woman's and the doctor's benefit. At no time should a male doctor examine a female patient in the absence of a chaperone unless it is a life-threatening situation.

The general assessment might quite correctly be concentrated on such aspects as:

- Signs of haemorrhage, anaemia
- Infection
- Suitability for general anaesthesia
- Distant signs of gynaecological disease (i.e. metastases)
- Signs of pregnancy
- Abnormal development (i.e. precocious puberty)
- Hirsutism
- Hypo- or hyperthyroidism
- Obesity, anorexia
- Galactorrhoea
- Emotional state

Abdominal examination

This examination should be performed with the woman lying flat, or semi-reclining if the former position provokes cardiorespiratory embarrassment. Details to note are shown in Table 1.2.

Sites of tenderness should be carefully documented and borne in mind with regard to the pelvic examination that should follow.

Just as in general surgery, a rectal examination should be considered in situations where a pelvic mass is suspected or where there is a history of disturbed bowel function or rectal bleeding.

Pelvic examination

Examination of the genitalia and pelvic examination usually form the basis of a thorough gynaecological assessment.

Table 1.2	Points to note during abdominal examination
Obesity	
Scars:	What surgery
	Why
	When
Movement:	Breathing
	Fetal movement
Distension:	Gas
	Fluid
	Solid tumours
	Pregnancy
Tenderness	
Peritonism	
Organomegaly	
Masses:	Size
	Shape
	Texture
	Position
	Fixity/mobility
	Tenderness
	? Pelvic in origin
Hernias	
Inguinal lymph nodes	

Position for examination

The appropriate position for examination is one of the following:

- Dorsal (woman lying on her back with knees flexed and thighs abducted)
- Left lateral
- Simms position (semi-prone)

(See also Table 1.3.)

The dorsal position is used most frequently and allows for a simple bimanual and speculum examination without having to change position. The left lateral and Simms are useful to assess vaginal prolapse. A careful explanation should be given to the woman before commencing the examination.

NOTE

Prior to pelvic examination the woman should:
- be comfortable
- have only the lower half of her body exposed
- be on an examination couch (hospital beds can often be too low)
- be well illuminated
- have an empty bladder *

* Unless there is a history of urinary incontinence, the woman should be asked to empty her bladder prior to the examination.

Inspection of the external genitalia
Details to look for are given in Table 1.3.

Should a smear be taken?
Prior to commencing the examination one should always make preparations to perform a cervical smear, particularly if:
- there is no record of a smear taken within the previous three years
- the woman has no recollection of having had a smear
- there are symptoms suggestive of a cervical problem (like postcoital bleeding)

The speculum examination
Normally the examination will begin with the woman in the dorsal position. The examiner should wear protective gloves. The external genitalia are inspected and the labia gently separated. The woman should be asked either to cough or to bear down.

Table 1.3 Inspection of the external genitalia	
Abnormalities of anatomy:	Cliteromegaly indicating virilism
	Signs of previous surgery
	Imperforate hymen
	Abnormal hair distribution
Changes in colouring:	White plaques (leukoplakia) indicating a skin disorder or pre-malignancy
	Erythema also seen in precancer but also inflammatory changes
	Hyperpigmentation or loss of pigment (vitiligo)
Signs of trauma:	Scratch marks indicate pruritus
Masses and ulceration:	Malignancy
	Genital warts
	Abscesses (i.e. Bartholin's)
	Herpes infection
Discharge:	May indicate vaginitis
Excoriation of labia or inner thighs:	May indicate urinary incontinence

This will demonstrate any stress incontinence and/or prolapse. If either are noted it will be necessary to perform a Simms speculum examination in the Simms position or in the left lateral position once the pelvic assessment has been completed.

There has always been some debate as to whether the bimanual, i.e. digital, examination of the vagina should be performed prior to insertion of a bivalve speculum. In most instances it is possible to select a speculum of appropriate dimensions without recourse to a digital examination. As a simple working rule:

- A speculum should not be inserted in women who have not commenced sexual activity as such examinations are painful and usually uninformative.

- A small Cusco's (size 2) should first be used in nulliparous patients or women who have not had a vaginal delivery.
- A larger speculum (size 3 or 4) may be used in women who have had vaginal deliveries.

There will always be exceptions where judgement should be excercised according to each case, for example:

- Women complaining of severe superficial dyspareunia (where an adequate assessment without recourse to anaesthesia may be impossible).
- Postmenopausal women where severe atrophic changes may make speculum insertion difficult and, despite their previous parity, a small speculum is required.
- Generally, children should never be examined without anaesthesia.

The speculum should be warmed and lubricated prior to insertion. A small amount of K-Y Jelly® does not significantly interfere with either the ability to take a good smear or in its interpretation.

The bivalve speculum should be slowly inserted fully into the vagina so that the closed blades come to rest in the posterior fornix. The blades are then gently opened under direct vision and the cervix should then be exposed. If the cervix is not fully visualised then the uterus may be retroverted, i.e. the cervix will be naturally directed anteriorly. In this situation, gently withdraw the speculum a few centimetres and redirect the closed speculum toward the anterior fornix. Once placed anteriorly the blades should once again be opened under direct vision.

If a smear is to be taken, then this is the point at which it should be done (see 'Taking a cervical smear' in Section 6).

The cervix and upper vagina should be inspected carefully and any abnormalities noted.

Abnormalities to look for during speculum examination

Polyps	Ectropion
Ulcers	Tumours
Lacerations	Congenital abnormalities
Discharges	

If the woman is using an intrauterine device as a method of contraception, the presence or absence of the threads should be documented. Heavy discharges may obscure the cervix. Cultures (bacterial and fungal) should be taken and an endocervical swab should also be cultured (chlamydia and gonococci). Following appropriate swabs, the discharge should be gently swabbed away with cotton-wool on sponge-holding forceps to allow a thorough inspection of the cervix. If contact bleeding is noted this should be documented along with any other features that might explain such an observation. These might include atrophic changes in menopausal women, severe inflammatory changes such as might accompany a *Trichomonas* infection, or a mass or ulcer that could indicate malignancy.

In some situations, the cervical os may be noted to be open and/or have products of conception lodged within the canal (incomplete abortion), or necrotic tumour may be seen (cervical cancer). Any such tissue should be gently removed by sponge-holding forceps and assessed histologically.

It is important that during insertion and opening of the blades of the speculum, signs of tenderness and discomfort are noted and if excessive the procedure should be stopped.

Having inspected the cervix, and taken a cervical smear if indicated, the speculum should be slowly withdrawn with the blades partially open to allow examination of the vaginal epithelium (look for signs of trauma, warts, discharge, subepithelial cysts). If the blades are held widely open this will cause discomfort.

Bimanual examination

Generally, this examination is also performed with the woman lying in the dorsal position. In nulliparous women it might only be possible to insert one finger into the vagina. Parous women can normally accommodate both the index and second finger of the examining hand. The other hand is placed on the lower abdomen. The cervix is first located and its consistency noted. Gentle lateral pressure on the cervix might cause discomfort. This is called cervical excitation and usually indicates acute irritation or fixity of the cervical ligaments.

This clinical sign may suggest one of the following:

- Haemoperitoneum (ectopic pregnancy)
- Acute or chronic pelvic inflammatory disease
- Endometriosis

Endometriosis usually involves the uterosacral ligaments which are either irregular, fixed and tender or can cause pain on anteroposterior movement of the cervix. In extreme cases of pelvic tenderness (remember the abdominal findings) it may be impossible to proceed further. Whilst the examination might be considered to be inconclusive, such acute tenderness is an important clinical sign and is definitely abnormal.

After palpation of the cervix one then proceeds to define the size and position of the uterus. If the uterus is anteverted this will be felt between the examining fingers in the anterior fornix pushing the uterus up toward the examining hand on the lower abdomen. A normal-sized uterus in the non-pregnant woman is about the size of a pear. It should be freely mobile and not tender to gentle palpation. Convention usually dictates that degrees of uterine enlargement are recorded in terms of weeks of pregnancy; thus, a uterus that is just palpable above the symphysis pubis would be described as approximately 12 weeks, whereas one reaching the umbilicus would be described as approximately 20 weeks. To discern whether a pelvic mass is uterine or adnexal, the mass (if mobile) should be moved. If this is accompanied by movement of the cervix then it is likely that the mass originates from the uterus. A mass such as an ovarian cyst is less likely to result in cervical movement unless of course it is fixed to the uterus.

Points to note on uterine palpation
Position (anteverted, retroverted or axial)
Size
Regularly or irregularly enlarged
Lateral deviation
Mobility
Tenderness
Consistency (soft or firm)

Apart from size, mobility and tenderness, the consistency and regularity of the uterus can be commented on; for example, a 12-week sized, firm and irregular uterus would suggest uterine fibroids, whereas a 12-week sized, soft and regularly enlarged uterus might suggest a pregnancy.

The adnexa refer to the tissues on either side of the uterus and are palpated by moving the hands laterally, having first located the uterus. Once again, the same criteria for describing masses are applied (20-week, smooth, mobile, non-tender cystic mass might suggest an ovarian cyst). Normal ovaries can sometimes be palpated in the premenopausal woman and they are usually tender if palpated with excess pressure. Any adnexal swelling in a postmenopausal woman should be considered as abnormal and is a justification for a more detailed assessment such as ultrasonography.

If the uterus is retroverted then it will not be possible to estimate the uterine size by bimanual palpation unless, of course, the position can be converted to one of anteversion. A smooth, globular swelling will be felt immediately behind the cervix in the pouch of Douglas. In retroversion, the long axis of the cervix will be directed towards the anterior vaginal wall.

Having completed the bimanual examination, if the history is suggestive of uterovaginal prolapse and/or the previous examination(s) have revealed signs of prolapse, a Simms speculum examination should be performed with the woman moved into either the left lateral or Simms (semi-prone) position. With the Simms speculum and a suitable instrument to gently retract and elevate the anterior vaginal wall the following should be noted:

- Cervical descent: Grade I (cervix descends to the level of the introitus)

  Grade II (cervix descends beyond the introitus but part of the uterus remains intravaginal)

  Grade III (complete procidentia, when all of the uterus descends beyond the introitus)

- Bulging of the anterior vaginal wall (cystocoele)
- Bulging of the posterior vaginal wall (rectocoele)
- Bulging of the posterior fornix (enterocoele)

In cases where a pelvic neoplasm is suspected or to aid in the differentiation of a rectocoele from an enterocoele, a combined rectal and vaginal examination should be performed.

DOCUMENTATION OF HISTORY AND EXAMINATION

Clear and concise notes are as important as the assessment itself. The date and time of the assessment should be recorded and if you are in doubt what to do next you should inform a more senior member of staff.

At the conclusion of a gynaecological examination your documentation should include all the points shown in Table 1.4.

Table 1.4 Points to be covered in documentation following interview

- What the presenting problem is
- Any associated problems
- What the likely diagnosis is (not a list of all possibilities)
- Any complicating issues, i.e. use of steroids or anticoagulants
- What investigations, if any, need to be done and have already been arranged
- What is planned to happen next, i.e. nil by mouth and for evacuation of uterus
- What information has been given to the woman, relatives and friends

COMMUNICATION WITH GPs AND OTHER PROFESSIONALS

Concise and accurate communication of information is as much a part of the doctor's role as is seeing and assessing patients. Letters to general practitioners should be written promptly, contain clear and brief information and should avoid both repeating information given by the referring doctor and irrelevant information. Once dictated, letters should be read, signed and sent as soon as possible. Many GPs complain of delay and this is clearly avoidable in the majority of situations. If results of investigations are outstanding then this can be stated in the letter, with the results and what they mean communicated at a later date.

There are situations where it is advisable to telephone the GP so that he or she may be informed of the situation prior to the woman being discharged. Examples of situations where the telephone should be used are:

- Stillbirth or early neonatal death
- Woman taking her own discharge
- Newly diagnosed malignant disease
- Inpatient death
- Concern regarding socio-domestic circumstances
- Likely home visit within 48 hours

OBTAINING CONSENT

All procedures require consent and the level at which one will obtain consent may vary according to local circumstances. In general, all procedures that will be performed under a general anaesthetic require the completion of a written consent form (the format will vary depending on the type of procedure and the local requirements).

Consent of legal guardians

Any procedure performed on a minor, or on an adult who is unable to give consent (severe mental retardation, unconscious, etc.), will require the consent of a legal guardian and in exceptional circumstances it may be necessary to apply to the court for permission to proceed.

Consent in unanaesthetised patients

Procedures performed on adults who are alert and conscious do not normally require written consent as this is implied. Nevertheless, there may also be exceptions to this. In some units written consent is required prior to examinations such as colposcopy, particularly if treatment is to be performed at the same time. The same may also apply to fitting and removal of an intrauterine device or the injection of depot contraceptives. It is always wise to check with your consultant which procedures, if any, performed on conscious patients will require written consent.

Ensuring the patient understands

It is as well to remember that most consent forms, as they are not witnessed by an independent authority, are not legal documents although obtaining proper INFORMED consent is regarded as good clinical practice and goes a long way to providing a meaningful and documented message that the patient agrees to the procedure named on the consent form, i.e. if there is a possibility of ovarian pathology at the time of hysterectomy this should be discussed in full with the woman and consent obtained for bilateral oophorectomy.

Special consent situations in gynaecology

There are some special situations in gynaecology that require a little more thought. Sterilisation procedures, although not technically requiring the consent of the woman's partner should, if possible, contain it, particularly if the woman and/or her partner so desire. Termination of pregnancy similarly does not require the partner's consent but should do so if the woman and her partner feel more comfortable with a joint decision.

A more difficult issue is consent for an examination under anaesthesia. This should be explained to the woman prior to obtaining consent and in most situations it is an essential part of the procedure. If, however, it is to be performed as part of a teaching exercise, e.g. medical students, this should be explained to the woman and some units require written consent for this also. Many authorities feel that this is part of good clinical practice and should the woman not wish to be examined under anaesthesia as part of clinical teaching, her wishes should be documented and respected.

If other procedures are to be performed alongside the main operation, these should be documented on the consent form. Insertion of suppositories does not normally require written consent if it has been adequately explained to the woman and is part of the standard procedure of that unit (i.e. Flagyl® or Voltarol®).

Blood transfusion

Finally, some women may not wish to have a blood transfusion. The woman will often be asked to sign a form prior to her operation that this is her express wish. Naturally, her wishes should be respected. If the surgeon responsible feels that such a procedure would be hazardous without the ability to transfuse, he or she should discuss this fully with the woman first. If the risk is considered to be too great, some surgeons may decide to avoid the operative procedure and manage the problem by an alternative method.

2 *Emergency admissions*

Unscheduled vaginal bleeding with or without abdomino-pelvic pain is the most common reason for referral as an emergency. The majority of these women are not severely ill, although physical and emotional distress is common. It is necessary to make a rapid assessment of the woman's needs and avoid long delays in the casualty department.

TRIAGE FOR GYNAECOLOGICAL EMERGENCIES

Critically ill

Clinical assessment and resuscitation should be carried out simultaneously. These women should be given priority over all other clinical activities at that time. There are certain emergency situations in gynaecology that carry major mortality risks unless dealt with promptly, e.g. ruptured ectopic pregnancy.

Acute but stable

- *Diagnosis very probable:* Admission and appropriate management should be arranged and provided.
- *Diagnosis uncertain:* Due to either an ambiguous history and/or clinical findings, admission, observation and further investigations should be advised and arranged.

Very stable

- Women with normal physical findings and negative serum β HCG can be discharged, having been given a full explanation and advice to return if necessary.

- Women should be given an outpatient appointment for appropriate investigations and follow up.
- General practitioners should be informed of their attendance.

Management for the critically ill gynaecological emergency

- Insert large intravenous (IV) cannula, or central line to monitor central venous pressure (CVP).
- Provide oxygen or airway if respiratory distress is present.
- Intravenous analgesia if in severe pain (remember opiates depress respiration therefore you may need to assist ventilation also).
- Resuscitation with fluids, plasma expanders, O-negative blood, etc.
- Foley catheter to monitor urine output.
- Full blood count (FBC), group and crossmatch and electrolytes are the basic blood investigations.
- Consider clotting factors if disseminated intravascular coagulation (DIC) or sepsis is suspected.
- Immediate surgery may be required in some of the cases.
- IV antibiotics if sepsis is suspected, broad spectrum and cover Gram negative organisms.
- Such women might be in renal failure, DIC, and septicaemic shock and may even need intensive care management.
- Do not give more than two units of plasma expander. Uncrossmatched blood may occasionally be required.

PREGNANCY-RELATED EMERGENCIES

(Always consider that the woman may be pregnant.)

History and examination

Consider these as probable diagnoses:

- **Miscarriage**
- **Ectopic pregnancy**
- **Molar pregnancy**
- **Urinary retention due to retroversion of a gravid uterus**

if any of the following are present:

- There is a history of a missed period.
- There has been, or is, a positive pregnancy test, β HCG.
- There is unscheduled vaginal bleeding with or without associated pain.
- The woman is shocked.
- Clinically there is peritonism.
- There is an enlarged uterus or a pelvic mass.
- The cervix is soft and/or dilating.
- There are palpable or visible products in the cervical os.

NOTE

(a) Pelvic inflammatory disease (PID) is very rare in pregnancy. Miscarriage (see below) may often be associated with severe pain; this relates to cervical dilatation and its presence is more likely to indicate an inevitable or incomplete abortion.

(b) Women who say that they cannot be pregnant because they have been sterilised might still be pregnant as the procedure has a failure rate. Furthermore, failed sterilisation is more likely to result in an ectopic pregnancy.

(c) Women who have had tubal surgery are at an increased risk of ectopic pregnancy.

(d) **Always suspect ectopic pregnancy in a shocked patient.**

EARLY PREGNANCY ACCIDENTS

Investigations

- *Urine/serum β HCG:* Most laboratories will perform a rapid assay. This is a sensitive biochemical indicator of pregnancy.
- *Pelvic ultrasonography:* Performed abdominally (needs full bladder) or transvaginally. This will confirm the presence of an intrauterine pregnancy (or pregnancies) and also the presence of a fetal heart. An adnexal mass and fluid in the pouch of Douglas might suggest an ectopic pregnancy **but is not diagnostic**.
- *Blood grouping:* Necessary in order to assess the need for anti-D prophylaxis.
- *Full blood count:* To assess any need for replacement, co-existent sepsis and/or DIC.

Additional investigations

- Clotting profile if DIC is suspected.
- Blood cultures if sepsis is suspected.
- Baseline urea, electrolytes and creatinine if renal compromise.
- Haemoglobin electrophoresis in Afro-Caribbeans if sickle state is not known.

See also Table 2.1 and Figure 2.1.

Uterine evacuation

Preparation for uterine evacuation

Most procedures are performed under general anaesthesia in the UK. The woman should be fully counselled prior to the procedure. Very heavy bleeding should be dealt with as a matter of urgency. See Table 2.2 for preparation procedure.

Table 2.1   Types of early pregnancy accident

Intrauterine pregnancy	Characteristics
Threatened abortion	Bleeding; viable fetus; cervix closed
Inevitable abortion	Bleeding; fetal heart may be present; cervix opening
Incomplete abortion	Bleeding; non-viable fetus; products partially expelled
Complete abortion	Confirmed recent pregnancy; empty uterus
Blighted ovum	Confirmed recent pregnancy; no identifiable fetus
Missed abortion	Pregnancy *in utero*; no fetal heart detected
Septic abortion	Any abortion accompanied by sepsis
Ectopic pregnancy	
Tubal pregnancy	Bleeding and/or pain; pregnancy in fallopian tube
Cornual pregnancy	Bleeding and/or pain; pregnancy in uterine cornu
Cervical pregnancy	Bleeding and/or pain; pregnancy in cervical canal
Abdominal pregnancy	Bleeding and/or pain; pregnancy in peritoneal cavity

Figure 2.1 Early intrauterine pregnancy bleeding: management algorithm

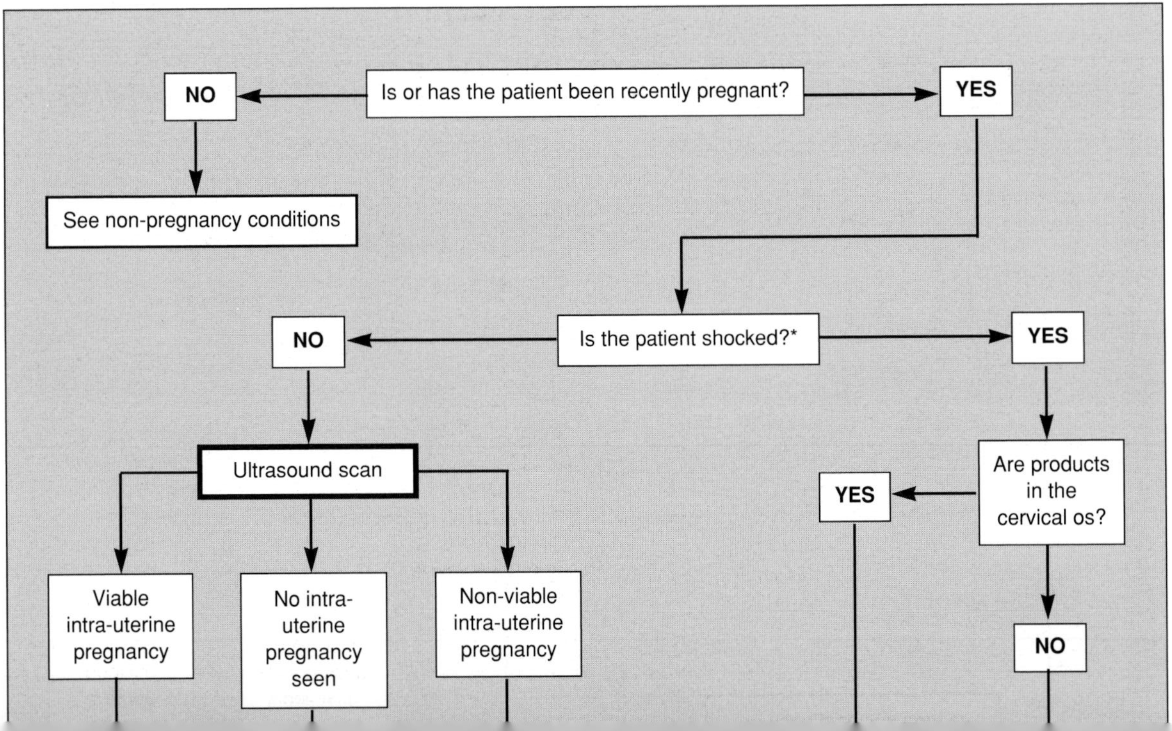

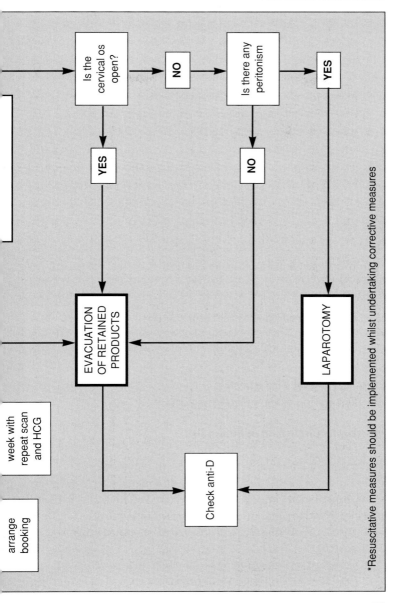

arrange
booking

week with
repeat scan
and HCG

Is the cervical os open?

YES

NO

EVACUATION OF RETAINED PRODUCTS

Is there any peritonism

NO

YES

LAPAROTOMY

Check anti-D

*Resuscitative measures should be implemented whilst undertaking corrective measures

23

Table 2.2 Preparation for uterine evacuation

- Nil by mouth.
- Check all necessary investigations are complete.
- Ensure consent (patient or legal guardian) has been obtained.
- Insert IV cannula and run in normal saline slowly.
- If bleeding is heavy add 20 units Syntocinon(r) to 1 l N saline and run in over one hour.
- If septic abortion is suspected intravenous antibiotics (broad spectrum to cover Gram negative organisms, e.g. gentamicin 120 mg IV stat), should be given for 24 hours prior to evacuation. These women are prone to septic shock, DIC and renal failure.

Note: In confirmed septic abortion the possibility of criminal interference should also be considered. Septic abortion is now uncommon. The women are usually very ill and bimanual examination may be impossible because of acute pain. There may be evidence of a purulent exudate; patients are generally pyrexial and the white cell count is raised.

Evacuation of the uterus

(See 'Evacuation of the uterus' in Section 6.)

Management after evacuation

Histological examination of products of conception

Different departments may have differing policies as to whether or not products of conception should be routinely assessed histologically. There are potential advantages in doing this:

- Detection of trophoblastic disease (if previously unsuspected)
- Confirms a conception (useful in infertility patients and in later assessment of recurrent miscarriage)

■ May reveal no chorionic tissue (raises the possibility of an extrauterine pregnancy or a complete miscarriage)*

* To differentiate between a complete miscarriage and a suspected extrauterine pregnancy one may either perform a laparoscopy or adopt a more conservative approach. In the latter, serum β HCG is monitored quantitatively: a sample is taken seven days after the evacuation; if this remains elevated or is rising, an ectopic pregnancy is more likely and a laparoscopy should be planned. Laparoscopy should also be performed if the woman continues to complain of pain.

Miscarriage aftercare

The blood loss should be monitored for six hours following evacuation. If bleeding remains heavy and/or the uterus enlarges, there are likely to be further retained products. An ultrasound scan may help but it may be difficult to differentiate between products and clot. If there is any doubt, a further exploration will be required.

■ Always check clotting status if the bleeding continues.
■ Counsel with regard to procedure and further pregnancies **when fully recovered from anaesthesia.**
■ Anti-D prophylaxis (see below).
■ If there has been excessive bleeding, check haemoglobin and give haematinics/transfuse as necessary.
■ In unplanned pregnancies, discuss family planning.

Most, if not all, women associate miscarriage with an enormous sense of loss and to some extent personal failure. Women – and their partners – should be offered miscarriage counselling if available. There are many local and national organisations that support self help in miscarriage.

The majority of patients are fit to be discharged home within 12 hours of evacuation. The GP should be informed and the woman given clear instructions to return if bleeding becomes heavier or she develops lower abdominal pain. She should be forewarned that some abdominal cramps may be experienced but these should be manageable by simple analgesics.

> **When talking to women after miscarrying some useful facts may be of help:**
> - Miscarriage occurs in about 1 in 7 pregnancies.
> - 50–60% are due to problems with the embryo/fetus.
> - 10–20% are due to problems with implantation.
> - In future pregnancies the risk is not increased.
> - A further pregnancy can be attempted when the woman feels fully adjusted and recovered.
> - Information booklets and support groups are available.

Anti-D immunoglobulin prophylaxis

It is necessary to administer anti-D immunoglobulin to all rhesus-negative women when during the pregnancy it is possible that sensitisation to the anti-rhesus-D antibody may have occurred (Figure 2.2).

SUSPECTED ECTOPIC PREGNANCY

A suspicion of an ectopic pregnancy is a common reason for referral to hospital. Not all of these women will have an ectopic pregnancy but the approach to management should always be with this in mind. The classic presentation of amenorrhoea, pain, slight vaginal bleeding and shock is rare now as many women will be referred prior to rupture of the tube. Bleeding from a ruptured corpus luteum is the most likely differential diagnosis; the management, however, will be similar in that the bleeding will have to be controlled.

History

- Amenorrhoea or unscheduled bleeding
- Other symptoms of pregnancy (breast tenderness, nausea, frequency)
- Lateralised pelvic pain
- Shoulder-tip pain (diaphragmatic irritation)

Figure 2.2 When and how much anti-D to administer?

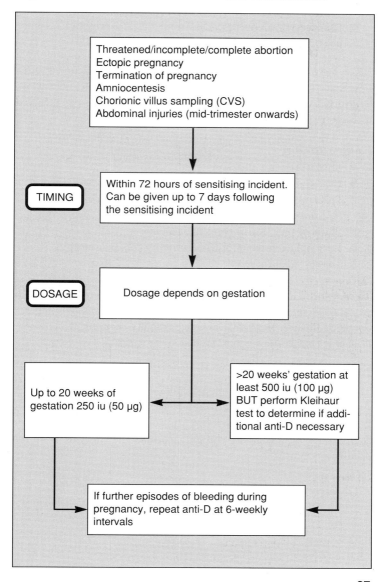

Threatened/incomplete/complete abortion
Ectopic pregnancy
Termination of pregnancy
Amniocentesis
Chorionic villus sampling (CVS)
Abdominal injuries (mid-trimester onwards)

TIMING — Within 72 hours of sensitising incident. Can be given up to 7 days following the sensitising incident

DOSAGE — Dosage depends on gestation

Up to 20 weeks of gestation 250 iu (50 µg)

>20 weeks' gestation at least 500 iu (100 µg) BUT perform Kleihaur test to determine if additional anti-D necessary

If further episodes of bleeding during pregnancy, repeat anti-D at 6-weekly intervals

- Recent positive pregnancy test
- IUCD use
- Past history of sterilisation, tubal surgery, previous ectopic, pelvic inflammatory disease

Note: Very few patients will fulfil all of these criteria; any, however, should raise the possibility of ectopic gestation. Examination and further investigations should be directed towards excluding/confirming the diagnosis.

Examination

- Shocked or not shocked
- Pyrexial (haemoperitoneum can cause a pyrexia)
- Peritonism (guarding and rebound may indicate haemoperitoneum)
- Signs of pregnancy (breasts, cervix)
- Cervical excitation (pain on moving cervix laterally)
- Tender adnexal mass*

* If there are sufficient grounds to suspect an ectopic pregnancy, palpation of the adnexa should be deferred until the woman is in the operating theatre. This is to avoid the possibility of rupturing a tubal pregnancy before the woman is prepared for surgery.

Investigations

These are the same as detailed for all early pregnancy accidents. In severely ill patients (see triage below), blood should be taken for crossmatching, haemoglobin and serum β HCG but management must be based on clinical grounds, i.e. do not wait for results.

TRIAGE FOR SUSPECTED ECTOPIC PREGNANCY

Critically ill patients

If severely ill, and shocked, this situation will require **laparotomy** and resuscitation. In cases of ectopic pregnancy it may be necessary to operate prior to resuscitation. Surgery should always be performed unless there is an obvious cause for shock that will not be surgically correctable.

Acute but stable

Any woman of childbearing age presenting with amenorrhoea, regardless of current family planning (including sterilisation) should have a β HCG performed. A pelvic ultrasound scan is also useful, not necessarily to visualise an ectopic pregnancy but to exclude an intrauterine pregnancy. An empty uterus in conjunction with an elevated β HCG should raise the possibility of an ectopic pregnancy. If pain is present plus either pelvic tenderness or a palpable adnexal mass, the woman should have an urgent laparoscopic assessment and be prepared for theatre.

Very stable

A further β HCG estimation should be performed in 3–5 days. Patients can be discharged but with instructions to both themselves and their GPs that any pain should prompt a reassessment either by the GP or in casualty.

In women where surgery is contemplated, preparation should be as for those with other early pregnancy accidents. The rules for rhesus isoimmunisation prophylaxis apply for ectopic gestation just as for miscarriage following intrauterine pregnancy. In women having laparoscopy as an initial diagnostic procedure, they should be counselled that laparotomy may be necessary and consent for such procedures should be obtained.

Summary of management of suspected ectopic pregnancy

Patient in severe pain or shocked

- IV cannula
- IV fluids or plasma expander if shocked
- Bloods for HCG, haemoglobin, group and crossmatch if shocked
- Consider O-negative blood
- Analgesia
- Laparoscopy or laparotomy

Patient stable but in pain and/or palpable pelvic mass

- IV cannula
- Serum/urine β HCG
- Haemoglobin
- Group and hold serum
- Analgesia as required
- Urgent pelvic ultrasound scan
- Laparoscopy if no intrauterine pregnancy
- If there is an intrauterine pregnancy treat as for threatened abortion. (Concurrent ectopic and intrauterine pregnancy occurs rarely.)

Patient stable, no or minimal pain, normal pelvic examination

- Serum/urine β HCG
- Pelvic ultrasound scan
- If no intrauterine pregnancy, repeat β HCG in 3–5 days

Confirmed tubal pregnancy

If tube is ruptured:
- Laparotomy and salpingectomy
- Check status of remaining tube and ovaries

If tube is unruptured:
- Laparoscopic or laparotomy salpingostomy

Note: Pregnancies that are ectopic but not involving the tube should be excised and the pelvic organs reconstructed if possible. In this situation removal of the conceptus and control of haemorrhage must be the primary consideration. Occasionally (e.g. cervical pregnancy extending into broad ligament), a hysterectomy may be necessary. If a bleeding corpus luteum is found to be the cause, then this can be oversewn. There is rarely, if ever, any need to remove the ovary.

Post-operative care
As soon as the woman is recovered sufficiently to understand and ask questions:
- Counsel with regard to the findings and procedure.
- Administer anti-D prophylaxis if indicated.
- Assess haemoglobin: iron supplementation or transfusion if indicated.
- Discuss future fertility (reduced by 20% – NOT 50%).
- Indicate increased risk of further ectopic pregnancy.
- Discuss family-planning needs (warn regarding IUCD and progesterone-only pills).
- Arrange follow-up for post-operative examination and further counselling.
- Check histology to confirm pregnancy and exclude trophoblastic disease.

PELVIC INFLAMMATORY DISEASE (PID)

This is probably the most frequent diagnosis for women presenting with lower abdominal pain. Only a minority of such women will actually have pelvic infection and because of the associated features (contact tracing etc.) and subsequent sequelae (infertility or subfertility), it is important to confirm the diagnosis and not 'label' a woman as having PID inaccurately.

What is PID?
- Pelvic peritonitis
- Oophoritis
- Salpingitis
- Endometritis

Causal organisms of PID
- *Chlamydia trachomatis* (50%)
- *Neisseria gonorrhoeae* (15–20%)
- Others (*E. coli*)
- Mixed infections

Note: Most infections are ascending infections following coitus with an infected partner.

Sequelae

If unrecognised or inadequately treated, PID may eventually result in:

- **Recurrent PID:** 25% of women develop a subsequent infection.
- **Infertility:** 12% are infertile after one infection.
  35% are infertile after two infections.
  70% are infertile after three infections.

- **Ectopic pregnancy:** Risk increased by a factor of six.
- **Chronic pelvic pain**
- **Dyspareunia**
- **Tubo-ovarian** Only 10% will achieve a successful
  abscess: pregnancy.

Spectrum of disease
- **Asymptomatic:** In some cases of PID documented at laparoscopy for unrelated reasons, there is no history at all.
- **Mild pain:** Vague lower abdominal pain as the only presenting feature.
- **Moderate pain:** Moderate pain, dyspareunia with or without a vaginal discharge.
- **Severe pain:** Peritonism, abscess formation rigors and high fever.

History
As the spectrum of disease is so wide, the history often reflects this. In a woman complaining of pelvic pain who **is not pregnant**, any of the following might indicate PID:
- Low abdominal pain
- Offensive and/or purulent vaginal discharge
- Deep and delayed dyspareunia
- Menstrual irregularity and/or dysmenorrhoea (secondary)
- A past history of ectopic pregnancy, IUCD use, or proven infection
- A history of involuntary infertility

Examination
- Pain ranges from mild lower abdominal tenderness to frank peritonism
- Pyrexia
- Cervical excitation
- Tender, fixed pelvic organs
- Adnexal masses

Investigations

If the history and examination are suggestive of PID the following investigations are useful:

- Full blood count with differential white cell count
- Sickle screen if indicated
- β HCG (see above)
- Mid-stream urine for culture and sensitivity
- Urine specimen for microscopy
- High vaginal swab for culture and sensitivity
- Endocervical swab for chlamydia, gonococci

In some circumstances the following must also be considered:

- Blood cultures (severely ill woman)
- Urethral, rectal and pharyngeal swabs (gonococci and/or chlamydia suspected).
  (*Note:* urethral swabs are uncomfortable for the woman.)
- Pelvic ultrasound (pelvic mass)

Diagnosis

Diagnosis may be made on clinical grounds using Hegar's criteria (Table 2.3).

Primary management

- The triage system should be applied.
- Should be considered as a multi-organism disease at the outset and single agent antibiotics are seldom if ever used.

Severely ill patients

- Admit
- Analgesia
- IV fluid replacement
- IV antibiotics
- Laparotomy and drainage if pelvic abscess present
- Surgical exploration with or without drainage if failure to

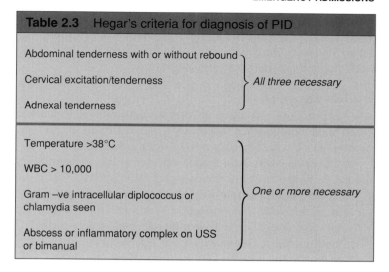

Table 2.3 Hegar's criteria for diagnosis of PID

Abdominal tenderness with or without rebound	
Cervical excitation/tenderness	*All three necessary*
Adnexal tenderness	
Temperature >38°C	
WBC > 10,000	
Gram –ve intracellular diplococcus or chlamydia seen	*One or more necessary*
Abscess or inflammatory complex on USS or bimanual	

respond to medical measures or symptoms persisting with negative bacterial cultures

Note: Useful first-line antibiotics include tetracyclines, metronidazole, cefuroxime, amoxycillin (with probenecid) and erythromycin. They can be altered appropriately once the results of bacteriological investigations become available.

Stable but ill patients

- Admit
- Analgesia and other supportive therapy as required
- Oral antibiotics when results of bacteriological investigations are available

Note: If no pathogens are isolated and spontaneous improvement occurs, these women should not be given a diagnosis of pelvic inflammatory disease. If no pathogens are isolated and the situation does not improve or deteriorates, laparoscopy should be considered (with swabs from the tubes if possible). If appropriate antibiotics are prescribed and the woman does not improve, then again consideration should be given to laparoscopy as there may be an undiagnosed ectopic or a pelvic collection or, indeed, an accident in an ovarian cyst (see below).

Minimal discomfort

After appropriate investigations, the woman may be discharged (with mild analgesics if necessary) and reviewed as an out-patient once the bacteriology results become available.

In all women who have had confirmed pelvic inflammatory disease there are three important aspects of follow-up:

- **Appropriate counselling and contact tracing** should be performed if the organism suggests a sexually transmitted disease. This may require referral to a department of genito-urinary medicine.
- **Subsequent fertility**. The possible effects should be discussed with particular emphasis on the increased likelihood of ectopic pregnancy.
- **Discharge back to primary care when cultures are negative for pathogens**. One cannot rely on an asymptomatic state to adequately exclude the presence of residual disease.

Further investigations in confirmed PID

The organisms most likely to cause pelvic inflammatory disease are *E. coli*, gonococci and *Chlamydia trachomatis* (CT). The latter two are always sexually transmitted. If an STD is suspected or confirmed, further actions required include:

- Cervical smear
- Serological tests for syphilis
- Specific tests, such as herpes culture, are indicated if sores are present, and HIV antibodies should only be measured after counselling.

Some notes on specimen taking

Failure to diagnose an STD is usually a result of incorrect specimen taking: the wrong site, the wrong medium or delay in getting the specimen to the laboratory.

Culturing gonococcus

The best specimens for gonococcus isolation are cervical secretions; urethral and rectal swabs may also grow gonococcus and should ideally be taken as well. Throat swabs are required if oral sex has taken place, especially if this may have been the only form of sexual activity, e.g. in prostitutes. A selective medium should be inoculated with the specimen to improve the chances of isolating the organism.

Culturing chlamydia

Chlamydia grows in epithelial cells of the cervix, so the cervical swab for CT needs to be taken vigorously in order to dislodge enough of these cells. *Chlamydia trachomatis* does not have a cell wall, which makes culture on normal media impossible. Cell culture, as for a virus, is available, along with several other antibody-mediated detection methods.

OVARIAN DISEASE

The major problems presenting as emergencies and related primarily to the ovary are:

- Torsion of ovarian cyst or ovary
- Haemorrhage into a cyst
- Rupture of a cyst
- Ovulation pain
- Postmenopausal cysts
- Hyperstimulation (infertility patients)

TORSION OF OVARIAN CYST OR OVARY

History

Torsion of the normal or cystic ovary causes acute pain, usually in the iliac fossae, although severe pain may be impossible to localise.

- Intermittent colicky iliac fossa pain (may be quite a long history)
- Vomiting
- Usually premenopausal
- Continuous, severe pain may indicate infarction
- Follicular and luteal cysts may produce steroid hormones resulting in menstrual disturbance prior to presentation

Examination

It may be possible to palpate an ovarian mass but if the pain is severe, pelvic examination may well be unrewarding.

Investigation

Investigation is aimed at excluding other conditions with similar presentations (e.g. ectopic, PID, etc.). Ultrasonography may demonstrate an adnexal cyst.

NOTE

(a) Torsion results initially in obstruction of venous return and stretching of the ovarian capsule. In advanced and neglected cases the whole appendage may infarct. If there is any doubt about the diagnosis, the woman should be prepared for laparoscopy with consent to proceed to laparotomy.

(b) In some instances the torsion can be corrected and the ovarian cyst, if present, removed, thus conserving ovarian function. This is important if the contra-lateral ovary is damaged or missing.

(c) All excised material should be histologically analysed.

HAEMORRHAGE INTO A CYST

This is another 'accident' that can occur with ovarian cysts. Bleeding from a ruptured corpus luteum may cause profound shock along with the signs of a haemoperitoneum similar to a ruptured ectopic pregnancy. The diagnosis is made by laparoscopy and/or laparotomy and the management by resuscitation and oversewing the bleeding point.

If haemorrhage occurs into a cyst there will be rapid distension of the capsule and associated pain. If shock is present it is usually due to the severe pain that can accompany such haemorrhage and not blood loss. Management is laparotomy and oophorectomy. **There is an increased risk of such cysts having malign elements and histology should be sought in all cases.**

RUPTURE OF A CYST

All types of ovarian cyst can rupture spontaneously and the resultant peritoneal irritation leads to an acute presentation. The symptoms may be quite mild to severe and either no obvious signs are present or those signs associated with peritonism and a pelvic mass. Ultrasound examination will reveal free fluid in the pouch of Douglas, especially if the cyst was large.

Dermoid cysts can occasionally rupture and the sebaceous contents are highly irritant. If there is any doubt regarding the diagnosis, a laparoscopy should be considered.

OVULATION PAIN

The onset of pain mid-cycle in a regularly menstruating woman is usually the clue to diagnosis.

Normal ovulating women will of course rupture a developing follicle approximately 14 days prior to menstruation. Very few women will present as an emergency because of ovulation although in young women it occasionally causes severe pain (and anxiety) and therefore presents as an emergency. There is usually very little if any constitutional upset and apart from tenderness on pelvic examination, no striking clinical signs.

Fluid may be seen in the pouch of Douglas and a collapsed follicle might also be visualised on ultrasound scan.

Management

Simple analgesics and reassurance are usually all that is required, although if pain persists for more than 48 hours a further assessment may be necessary. Women who have recurrent ovulation pain (mittelschmerz) can be managed by ovulation suppression with combined oral contraception.

POSTMENOPAUSAL CYSTS

Ovarian malignancy is much more common in postmenopausal women. Any suspected ovarian mass or acute presentation thought to result from such a mass requires both primary management and thorough investigation.

A woman presenting with a pelvic mass in this age group should only be managed by emergency surgery if severely ill and a life-saving procedure is required. In all other circumstances a thorough pre-operative evaluation should be performed (see 'Pelvic mass' in Section 5) and surgery planned electively at a time where a gynaecologist trained in the appropriate surgery is available.

OVARIAN HYPERSTIMULATION SYNDROME (OHSS)

This is an iatrogenic condition. It is a side-effect of infertility treatment, usually gonadotrophins (FSH/LH), either on their own or with HCG administration or in combination with gonadotrophin hormone releasing hormone analogue (GnRH-a) in superovulation regimes for assisted conception treatments. Rarely, this condition can occur after clomiphene (usually in a woman with polycystic ovarian syndrome) and gonadotrophin hormone releasing hormone (GnRH).

Any woman undergoing infertility treatment is at risk but there are certain factors which increase the risk:

- Polycystic ovarian disease
- Use of GnRH analogues and gonadotrophins in assisted conception cycles
- Luteal phase support with HCG
- Conception cycles

For a classification of OHSS, see Table 2.4.

Initial investigations

- FBC and platelets
- Biochemical profile – total protein, serum albumin, urea and electrolytes, creatinine
- Coagulation screen
- Group and save serum
- Chest X-ray – if pleural effusion suspected
- Ultrasound scan – twice weekly to determine ovarian size and extent of ascites
- Pregnancy test
- Consider blood gases if dyspnoea/tachypnoea severe

Complications

- Haemoconcentration – due to hypovolaemia as a result of ascites/pleural effusion, etc.
- Cardiorespiratory – due to ascites/abdominal distension/ pleural effusion/pericardial effusions
- Thromboembolism – due to haemoconcentration
- Renal failure – due to decreased perfusion/hypovolaemia
- Ovarian – torsion/haemorrhage/rupture
- Adult respiratory distress syndrome (ARDS)

Treatment for OHSS

Mild
Observation
Woman may stay at home
Review weekly with ultrasound scan

Moderate
Can be managed at home
If nausea and vomiting is a problem, will need admission
for IV fluids
Weekly scans for measurement of ovaries and ascites

Severe
Admission to hospital essential as this can be fatal.
- Rest and observation
- Daily girth measurements
- Daily weight measurements
- Strict fluid balance – daily intake and output charts
- Temp/pulse/BP – 4-hourly
- Maintain circulatory blood volume – intake of 3 l/day by
  mouth +/– IV fluids. Type of IV fluid will be governed by
  degree of haemoconcentration. A crystalloid (i.e.
  normal saline) is commonly used, although this risks
  making the ascites/pleural effusion worse.
- Close monitoring of serum potassium is also necessary.
  Colloids maintain circulatory blood volume better than
  crystalloid. If Hb concentration >16 g/dl, haematocrit
  >44% and serum albumin concentration <30 g/l
  albumin should be given. An isotonic 4.5% solution of
  albumin can be given over 2–4 hours. If circulating
  blood volume is markedly depleted, women will be olig-
  uric, hypotensive and have a tachycardia – in this situation CVP monitoring is necessary.
- Cardiorespiratory – if dyspnoea becomes severe, consid-

eration must be given to drainage of pleural effusions and ascites.

- Pericardial effusions – manage conservatively.
- Tense ascites should be drained under ultrasound control to avoid damage to ovaries. Abdominal paracentesis is advised. Drain can be left in for several days. Drainage of ascites can simultaneously improve renal function. IV albumin should be given at the time of abdominal paracentesis to maintain blood volume.
- Thromboembolism – TED stockings, s.c. heparin – prophylactic – if severe, hyperstimulation
- Oliguria/renal failure – catheterise – hourly urine measurements
- Maintain circulating blood volume
- Albumin infusions to correct haemoconcentration
- Avoid diuretics
- Consider dopamine if alternative measures are failing

Ovarian complications

- If torsion/haemorrhage/rupture are suspected laparotomy is necessary. Management should be conservative.

If ARDS is suspected, transfer to intensive care unit
Termination of pregnancy should be considered only under extreme circumstances when the woman's life is threatened

Pain relief
Paracetamol/co-dydramol
Occasionally opiates are necessary

Nausea/vomiting
Metoclopromide (IM or suppositories)
Stemetil®
There appears to be no benefit in prescribing non-steroidal anti-inflammatory drugs (NSAIDs).

Table 2.4 Classification of OHSS

Severity	Size of ovaries on ultrasound	Symptoms	Clinical/laboratory findings
Mild	Ovaries slightly enlarged, 5–8 cm	Abdominal discomfort; abdominal bloating; nausea	Enlarged ovaries on palpation (or nil palpable)
Moderate	8–10 cm	Abdominal discomfort; nausea and vomiting	Abdominal distension; tenderness and ascites
Severe	>10 cm	Abdominal discomfort; nausea and vomiting; dyspnoea, oedema and cough	Ascites; pleural effusion; haemoconcentration; hypoproteinaemia; coagulation abnormalities

MOLAR PREGNANCY

See under 'Trophoblastic disease' in Section 5.

POSTMENOPAUSAL BLEEDING

This is not a common problem encountered in casualty and when it does arise it is usually because the bleeding is either very heavy or associated with other symptoms.

- A shocked patient should be managed by admission and blood replacement.
- A speculum examination and bimanual examination should be performed as the likely cause of heavy bleeding in this age group is a malignancy.
- If any tissue is seen in the vagina this should be sent for histological assessment.
- There is rarely, if ever, any need for diagnostic surgical intervention as an emergency procedure but all of these women will require further investigation as a matter of some urgency. These investigations should include:

1 A cervical smear, if the bleeding is not heavy
2 An endometrial sample
3 A pelvic and endometrial ultrasound assessment
4 If either (2) or (3) above is abnormal, hysteroscopy and formal curettage of the endometrium and endocervix should be carried out.

In all but the most severe cases of postmenopausal bleeding, investigations can be conducted as an outpatient on an urgent/elective basis.

A rare cause of bleeding in this age group is bleeding provoked by intercourse, particularly if sexual activity has recently been commenced or recommenced. Signs of trauma may be apparent. If necessary surgery may be required to repair lacerations. In lesser degrees of trauma, reassurance and prescribing a topical oestrogen cream is all that is required. If there is any doubt with regard to the source of bleeding, the woman should be thoroughly investigated to exclude the possibility of a malignancy.

DYSMENORRHOEA

Women who present as a result of pain may have dysmenorrhoea with no acute pathology (e.g. ectopic pregnancy, pelvic infection) to account for the presentation. Most presentations will occur in the young, although older women with conditions such as endometriosis or PID may also experience dysmenorrhoea. The latter will usually be secondary, i.e. they will have had normal periods prior to the event. The younger patients are more likely to have primary dysmenorrhoea.

The diagnosis can usually be made from the history in that pain will have occurred with or slightly prior to a normal or heavy menstrual loss.

■ Clinical examination is unlikely to add anything apart from the fact that no abnormal masses are present. The uterus might be tender (especially if endometriosis is the cause).

- Women rarely require admission and can be managed by simple analgesics.
- Prostaglandin synthetase inhibitors such as mefenamic acid are useful.
- In very severe cases the woman may require an opiate and admission.
- There is rarely any necessity to institute investigations on an emergency basis. Women with severe secondary dysmenorrhoea, which is more often associated with pelvic pathology, should be offered outpatient review. Primary dysmenorrhoea is best referred back to the woman's general practitioner with advice to consider combined oral contraception if the condition becomes chronic.

MENORRHAGIA

Only in severe cases of menstrual blood loss is an emergency presentation likely. However, there are situations when menorrhagia can be so severe as to warrant admission and transfusion.

Other causes of heavy vaginal bleeding need to be excluded, particularly pregnancy-related complications. The history may reveal that menorrhagia has been present for some time. Examination is necessary to exclude malignancies and fibroids, both of which can present in this way.

High-dose oral progestogens (norethisterone 10 mg t.d.s.) and bed rest usually result in an improvement but further outpatient assessment is desirable as endometrial sampling will be required, and arrangements for follow-up should be made.

There is rarely any need to instigate investigations in the emergency department.

GENITAL TRAUMA

Vaginal bleeding in any age group may be the result of trauma. Trauma may have been accidental or as a result of sexual attack or abuse. If rape or abuse is suspected a **senior member** of the medical staff should be informed immediately, especially if the patient is a child. (See 'Management of sexual assault and rape' below.)

- Trauma occurs affecting mainly the vulva.
- Sharp objects may penetrate the vagina and surrounding adjacent structures.
- Vulval haematomas can occur from falling astride a blunt object.
- Pain may be severe.
- Small haematomas can generally be controlled relatively easily with pressure and an ice pack.
- Larger haematomas require surgical incision and drainage and bleeding points may require ligation. Blood replacement may be required.
- Penetrating injuries of the vagina require examination under anaesthesia; superficial injuries are not serious but deep lacerations may involve the bladder, rectum or peritoneal cavity and prompt action is essential.
- Tetanus booster should be administered where immunisation is in date. However, antitoxin should be considered if evidence of immunisation is lacking.

VAGINAL BLEEDING IN CHILDREN

(Always call a senior staff member.)

Vaginal bleeding is abnormal before the age of nine years. It is a cause of major concern to parents, particularly if it is the result of trauma where abuse might be considered as a possibility.

Causes of vaginal bleeding in children
- Foreign body in the vagina
- Poor hygiene
- Sexual assault
- Sexual precocity
- Tumours, e.g. sarcoma botryoides

NOTE
- Parental consent is a must and at least one parent should be present during the initial examination. Full examination is best done under general anaesthetic.
- Pubertal menorrhagia usually responds well to hormone therapy (combined contraceptive pill) once any other pathology is ruled out.

VULVAL SWELLING OR PAIN

BARTHOLIN'S CYSTS OR ABSCESSES

These are the most common vulval problems presenting in casualty. In cases of abscess formation there may or may not be a pre-existing history of a Bartholin's cyst. The glands are bilateral but only rarely are both involved. They are sited at the postero-lateral aspects of the introitus. The gland and duct are located deep in the posterior third of each labia majora. Obstruction of the main duct results in retention and cystic dilatation, and secondary infection will result in abscess formation.

Symptoms
- Pain
- Tenderness
- Dyspareunia – the surrounding tissues will be inflamed and oedematous

Signs
- Posterior vulvo-vaginal swelling (may be fluctuant)
- Erythema
- May be evidence of pointing (abscess)

Differential diagnosis

Bartholin's cysts and abscesses are most commonly confused with simple vaginal mucus retention cysts, or on the vulva with localised sepsis of sweat glands or hair follicles. Most of the latter can quite easily be drained under local anaesthesia.

Management

Primary treatment consists of drainage by marsupialisation (see Section 6), which preserves gland function, and treatment with the appropriate antibiotic. The gonococcus may be an aetiological factor in infection and endocervical, anal and urethral swabs should be taken for culture.

In postmenopausal women an enlarged gland should raise the possibility of malignancy and a biopsy is indicated.

ACUTE VULVOVAGINITIS

This is most often due to herpes simplex virus and can produce severe pain. If there is urethral involvement it may also be associated with acute urinary retention. The diagnosis is based upon the appearance of vesicles, which form flat, non-indurated ulcers, 2–5 mm in diameter. They are exquisitely tender and painful. Adequate analgesia and acyclovir cream alleviate the symptoms. If urethral involvement prevents micturition, urethral catheterisation should be avoided and a suprapubic catheter may be necessary.

In severe cases it may be necessary to admit the woman, particularly if micturition is compromised.

HYPEREMESIS GRAVIDARUM

This is still a relatively common reason for emergency hospital referral. Most women will experience some degree of upper gastrointestinal disturbance in early pregnancy and this usually subsides by the beginning of the second trimester. In a few cases vomiting can be quite severe, resulting in diminished calorie and fluid intake. This results in ketosis and dehydration. The frequent retching can cause abdominal discomfort and general malaise. In extreme cases haematemesis occurs because of oesophageal tears.

The cause of hyperemesis is unknown but situations where the β HCG level may be abnormally raised, e.g. multiple pregnancy and molar pregnancy, seem to be more frequently associated with hyperemesis.

In mild cases reassurance and dietary advice (small, bland, calorific meals plus non-carbonated fluids) may suffice. In women who are either dehydrated or ketotic, admission with IV fluid replacement is necessary. Initially, simple electrolyte replacement for 48 hours is all that is required. Losses should be replaced and maintained by careful fluid balance management. Non-carbonated oral fluids can be allowed. If nausea and/or vomiting persists, an anti-emetic such as cyclizine can be commenced and given on a regular basis until oral fluids can be tolerated.

If there is no response to these simple measures, it may be necessary to consider parenteral nutrition until the spontaneous resolution of nausea occurs (although this is rare). Thyroid dysfunction can occasionally result in hyperemesis.

Useful investigations in women with hyperemesis
- Urine for ketones
- Mid-stream urine (? asymptomatic bacturia)
- Urea and electrolytes
- Serum β HCG
- Pelvic ultrasound scan
- Thyroid function

Initial inpatient management
- Bed rest
- IV fluid and electrolyte replacement

- Monitor fluid balance
- Anti-emetics
- Clear fluids only by mouth

MANAGEMENT OF SEXUAL ASSAULT AND RAPE

Rape is one of the major violent crimes and has tremendous impact on the woman's life. Of all rapes, 80–90% still go unreported. **Always inform a senior member of staff.**

Definition

Rape is an act of forced coitus without the victim's consent. Statutory rape is sexual activity with a female below the age of consent or with one who is unable to give consent due to disability, drug or alcohol influence and/or mental handicap.

It is essential to realise the legal and medical implications and obtain a detailed history. The history should be recorded in the woman's own words in the presence of a female chaperone.

History to be obtained in cases of sexual assault/rape
- Time, date and place of assault
- Amount, type and threat of force
- Whether vaginal penetration occurred
- Whether any foreign objects were used and where
- Description of the assailant: height, weight (approx.), race, hair colour, identifying features and if known/unknown to the woman
- Gynaecological history of the victim, especially LMP, contraception, most recent voluntary intercourse before the assault
- Alcohol and/or drug use and time and quantity used
- History of previous injuries
- Obtain informed consent from the woman regarding the proposed examination, collection of evidence, including possible photographs and treatment

---

Physical examination

The following should be documented:

- General appearance – condition of clothing, hair, emotional state
- Any visible injuries – site, nature (scratches, bites, echymoses, haematomas). If the woman refuses to have photographs taken, diagrammatic documentation can be made.
- Evidence of semen – semen will fluoresce under ultraviolet lamp. Wood's lamp (often used in the emergency rooms to detect corneal aberrations) can be used for this purpose in a darkened room.

To be collected from the woman:
- Clothes, including underpants
- Saliva, fingernails and hair for comparison

External genitalia examination

The following should be documented:

- Presence of bruising/laceration
- Presence or absence of blood, semen over the perineum
- State of the hymen should be recorded
- Any dried-up secretions can be gently wiped with a sterile gauze piece soaked in saline and sealed in labelled plastic containers for comparison and analysis

Speculum examination

- Vaginal lacerations, abrasions, bruises should be noted
- Swabs from vagina and cervix for gonococcal and chlamydial cultures
- Wet mount from the vaginal pool to determine the presence/absence of motile/non-motile sperms
- Smears from the vaginal pool which are allowed to air-dry can be used to identify ABO antigen and acid phosphate estimation

Medical management/prophylaxis of sexual assault and rape

Sexually transmitted diseases

- Procaine penicillin G 4.8 million units IM with oral probenecid

  or

- 3 g of oral Amoxil® with 1 g oral probenecid
- Doxycycline (oral) 100 mg daily × 7 days can be added with 200 mg on the first day

In women allergic to penicillin:

- Spectinomycin 2 g IM with doxycycline (oral) 100 mg daily × 14 days should be given to cover incubating syphilis. 200 mg should be given as a loading dose on Day 1

  or

- Tetracycline 1.5 g oral stat followed by 500 mg 6 hrly × 4 days. Tetanus prophylaxis if indicated.
- If known to be exposed to hepatitis B, immunoglobulin should be given.

Pregnancy

Postcoital contraception using 2 × 50 µg COCs taken 12 hours apart. These are notorious for causing nausea and vomiting and may harm a pre-existing pregnancy. Medical termination with RU486 can be offered if conception occurs.

Psychological support

This is very important. Referral to support groups or professional counsellor should be advised and arranged.

Follow-up

Medical and psychological follow-up is necessary according to laboratory results and treatment, and these should be arranged.

Bimanual examination

- Size, position of the uterus (? pre-existing pregnancy), adnexal mass, tenderness

Other laboratory tests

- Serum for syphilis, hepatitis B. These should be repeated six weeks later
- Serum β HCG. This should be repeated weekly till positive or the start of a period
- Blood group and rhesus
- Drug/alcohol level if indicated
- Urine analysis, including presence of semen
- Optional HIV testing – this should be repeated three-monthly for up to one year

3 *Elective admissions*

Day surgery

Many minor and intermediate procedures can be performed without recourse to an overnight stay in hospital. There are several protocols for day surgery both locally based and also generated by professional bodies such as the Royal Colleges. Most women having minor procedures under general anaesthesia are suitable for day-case surgery.

Cases unsuitable for day-case surgery
- Concurrent heart or chest disease
- Other major medical problems, e.g. diabetes, bleeding diathesis
- Certain drug usage, e.g. anticoagulants or steroids
- Previous adverse reaction to general anaesthesia
- The very elderly or infirm
- Poor social conditions
- No adult support available on discharge
- Grossly obese

When women are offered day-case admission in the outpatient department a simple checklist should be completed to ensure that the criteria for admission are met (each hospital should ideally have its own criteria). Under ideal circumstances, a pre-operative assessment should be made in the clinic so that on the day of admission minimal medical input is required. If women have been waiting for longer than three months it may be necessary to repeat the pre-operative physical check and repeat a haemoglobin estimation. Women of Afro-Caribbean origin should have their sickle status assessed prior to general anaesthesia.

All patients, whether day cases or full admissions, should be instructed to starve (food and fluids) for a minimum period of six hours prior to planned general anaesthesia.

When is menstruation a problem?

Menstruation is not a contraindication for surgery unless the procedure involves hysteroscopy and endometrial resection, or a cold knife cone biopsy. Increased intravasation of fluid can occur during resection and if CO_2 is used for diagnostic procedures, the gas bubbles that form will hinder vision. Laparoscopic assessments for infertility should be planned in the luteal phase and are generally best avoided during menstruation.

Rapid assessments of day-case admissions

A useful schedule for assessing day cases on admission is given in Table 3.1.

Full elective admissions

Women will require admission either because the criteria for day surgery are not met or the procedure planned will entail a period of recovery in hospital. Most major gynaecological procedures will not be able to go home on the same day as the operation is performed, although many can be admitted on the morning of surgery having starved from the previous evening (morning cases) or had only a light breakfast (afternoon cases).

A full history and examination should be performed. Speculum and bimanual examination should also be performed unless the woman has had a recent assessment, i.e. within three months.

Table 3.1 Schedule for assessment of day cases on admission

Document reason for admission:

- Is the situation the same as it was when assessed in outpatients?

- Is the woman fully aware of why surgery is being performed?

- Has there been any intercurrent illness since OPD assessment?

Are the local day-case criteria satisfied?

Are essential pre-operative investigations complete?

- Haemoglobin within three months

- Chest X-ray if indicated

- ECG if indicated

- Sickle status where indicated

Could the woman be pregnant?

Rapid β HCG if missed period, particularly if being sterilised or having fertility investigations

Is the woman menstruating?

Is the woman using any medication?

Time the woman last ate and drank.

Are there any known allergies?

Has consent been obtained?

Although the partner's consent may be obtained for sterilisation it is not mandatory.

If the patient is a minor, has the legal guardian consented?

> ### Procedures for major gynaecological surgery
> - Full explanation of procedure
> - Written consent (remains valid for three months)
> - Thromboprophylaxis as indicated (see below)
> - Antibiotic prophylaxis (see below)
> - Serum for blood group and save
> - Crossmatch as indicated (see below)
> - Urinalysis
> - MSU as indicated
> - Full blood count
> - Urea and electrolytes (see below)
> - Bowel preparation (see below)
> - Pubic shave (varies according to consultant preference)
> - Notes complete, i.e. all relevant reports filed
> - X-rays etc. available

Before termination of pregnancy

- **Documentation**

  It is essential for legal reasons that the pre-operative documentation ('Blue Form') has been completed and signed by two medical practitioners.

- **Cervical preparation**

  Some units employ a cervical softening procedure prior to suction TOP. This can be achieved by inserting a prostaglandin pessary into the posterior fornix one hour prior to planned surgery.

- **Assess rhesus status**

  Anti-D (250 iu) is required in rhesus-negative women.

- **Prophylaxis against infection**

  There is an increased risk of developing pelvic inflammatory disease following TOP (approx. 2%). This risk increases to 10% if the woman already has chlamydial infection (asymptomatic). The options are to screen all women undergoing TOP for sexually transmitted disease or giving prophylactic antibiotics. Oxytetracycline, 250 mg q.d.s. for seven days is suitable prophylaxis against developing chlamydial PID.

Before sterilisation

Always ensure that patients are not pregnant. Any woman who could be pregnant should have a pregnancy test performed. Ideally, the procedure should be performed in the follicular phase of the cycle, i.e. prior to ovulation. This is not always practical.

If an IUCD is removed at the time of the sterilisation, the woman should be advised to use alternative contraceptive measures until the time of the next period, particularly if the procedure has been performed in the second half of the cycle. If an IUCD is to be removed, it is also advisable to abstain from intercourse for five days prior to removal.

Some pre-operative procedures/investigations will vary according to the procedure and by local variations. A simple chart for most of the common procedures is shown in Table 3.2.

Chest X-rays
- Known cardiac or respiratory problems
- Recent respiratory tract infection
- Known or suspected malignancy

Some anaesthetic departments will have a policy of requiring chest X-rays prior to general anaesthesia in women above a certain age. Check with your anaesthetist.

Electrocardiograms
Similar criteria apply as for chest X-rays. Women who are hypertensive, have known cardiac disease, or are >60 years should also have an ECG.

Biochemical profiles
- Known or suspected renal or hepatic dysfunction
- Pelvic mass (possible effect on renal function)

Table 3.2 Common pre-operative procedures

	TAH ±BSO	Vaginal hyst.	Incont. surgery	Tubal surgery	Pelvic mass (benign)	Radical hyst.	Pelvic mass (?malig.)
Consent	Yes	Yes	Yes	Yes	Yes	Yes	Yes
Starve	Yes	Yes	Yes	Yes	Yes	Yes	Yes
FBC	Yes	Yes	Yes	Yes	Yes	Yes	Yes
Profile	Optional	No	Yes	No	Yes	Yes	Yes
Group	Yes	Yes	Yes	Yes	Yes	Yes	Yes
X-match	Optional	No	No	No	Optional	Yes – 4 units	Yes – 4 units
CXR	Optional	Optional	Optional	Optional	Optional	Yes	Yes
IVU	Optional	No	Optional	No	Yes	Yes	Yes
ECG	Optional	Optional	Optional	Optional	Optional	Yes	Yes
Tumour markers	No	No	No	No	Optional	No	Yes
MSU	No	Optional	Yes	No	Yes	Yes	Yes
Proph. antibiotics	Yes	Yes	Yes	Optional	Yes	Yes and post-op.	Yes and post-op.
Proph. anticoags	Optional	Optional	Optional	Optional	Yes	Yes and post-op.	Yes and post-op.
TEDs	Yes	Yes	Yes	Yes	Yes	Yes	Yes
Bowel prep.	Limited	Limited	Limited	Limited	Full	Full	Full
Stoma counsel	No	No	No	No	Optional	Optional	Yes
Pubic shave	Optional	Optional	Optional	Optional	Optional	Optional	Optional

- Anticipated prolonged post-operative bowel dysfunction
- Cachexia and/or ascites
- Diuretics
- Nausea and vomiting
- Baseline measurement in women scheduled to have transcervical resection of the endometrium (TCRE)

Screening for haemoglobinopathies

All non-Caucasians should have their sickle status assessed if not already known. Anaemic women of southern European origin should be investigated for other haemoglobinopathies.

Group and save

In addition to the procedures tabulated the following procedures should have blood grouped and saved:

- Suction TOP
- TCRE
- Myomectomy
- Knife cone biopsy
- Colposuspension

Drugs

A thorough history of current *and recent* drug usage should be taken. Drugs that affect coagulation, respiratory function and corticosteroids are important.

- **Oral anticoagulants**

  These should be stopped at least 48–72 hours before surgery and changed over to IV or subcutaneous (s.c.) heparin as necessary. Coagulation should be assessed at least four hours prior to planned surgery.

- **Oral contraceptives**

  These and other oestrogen preparations should be stopped at least four weeks prior to major surgery. In minor surgery without other concurrent risks of thromboembolism, oral contraceptives can be continued.

■ **Other drugs**

Tranquillisers, anti-depressants and other sedative-type drugs (including anti-convulsants) are important for anaesthetic purposes, as some may be incompatible with anaesthetic agents.

■ **Bronchodilators**

Asthmatics should be maintained on their bronchodilators and spirometry performed pre-operatively.

■ **Steroids**

Women using steroids should have additional steroid cover for their surgery (hydrocortisone IM on the morning of surgery).

IDENTIFICATION AND PERIOPERATIVE MANAGEMENT OF HIGH-RISK PATIENTS

Diabetes

All patients admitted for surgery should have their urine screened for glucose. If a woman is a known diabetic, an assessment of the adequacy of control should be made. Whilst an inpatient, the blood sugar should be regularly monitored by stick testing six-hourly.

Non-insulin-dependent diabetics

Non-insulin-dependent diabetics should ideally be changed over to a suitable insulin regimen prior to major surgery. For minor procedures in women on sulphonylureas and a fasting blood glucose of <8 mmol:

■ Omit drug on day of surgery
■ Monitor blood glucose
■ Avoid IV dextrose
■ Restart medication when eating

Insulin-dependent diabetics

■ Admit the day before surgery

- Arrange to be first on the list to minimise fasting
- 5% dextrose should be commenced at 8 a.m.
- Routine daily insulin should *not* be given
- Insulin (Actrapid®) infusion (plain) can be given by a sliding scale to maintain the blood sugar levels between 4 and 7 mmol
- Close monitoring of blood sugar and potassium levels is important until the woman is able to take care of her diet and insulin requirements

Cardiac valvular disease

Prophylaxis against bacterial endocarditis

Ampicillin 2 g IV 30 min before and 8 hours after the first dose with gentamicin 1.5 mg/kg body weight IV 30 min before and 8 hours after the first dose.

Penicillin allergy: Vancomycin 1 g over 100 min IV with gentamicin 1.5 mg/kg body weight IV 30 min before and 8 hours after first dose.

Anticoagulation

Patients who have had a valve replacement may be on long-term oral anticoagulants with warfarin. These patients should be switched over to IV/s.c. heparin at least 48 hours before surgery (and check INR).

Respiratory problems

Patients with chronic bronchitis or obstructive airways disease may need pulmonary function tests and blood gas studies. Physiotherapy and postural drainage should be started before and continued during the post-operative period.

PRE-OPERATIVE PROPHYLAXIS

DVT prophylaxis

- **High-risk patients**
  - ○ Graduated compression stockings
  - ○ Adjusted dose heparin 3500 u every 8 hours, starting 48 hours pre-op and maintained for five days (to maintain APTT between 1.5 and 2.5 × control) (once-daily fractionated heparins are an alternative)
- **Intermediate-risk patients**
  - ○ Graduated compression stockings
  - ○ Low-dose heparin (5000 u b.d. or 10 000 u b.d. if weight >90 kg), continued until ambulatory or discharged
- **Low-risk patients**
  - ○ Graduated compression stockings
- **Day cases** (>1 risk factor but insufficient to warrant full admission)
  - ○ Graduated compression stockings
  - ○ 1000 ml dextran 40 infused over six hours

A useful checklist of risk factors for DVT is given in Table 3.3.

Antibiotic prophylaxis

It is now well established that prophylactic antibiotics prevent post-operative infection and should be administered prior to skin incision and for not more than 48 hours unless the procedure itself may have increased the risk of intra-abdominal sepsis, e.g. bowel may have been opened. Usual drugs of choice are cefuroxime (750 mg at induction) and metronidazole (1 g PR, 1 hour pre-operation) or Augmentin®.

In women who are sensitive to penicillin, metronidazole 1 g PR, 1 hour pre-operatively and 80 mg gentamicin IV at induction is a suitable substitute.

Bowel preparation

Routine full bowel preparation is not necessary unless the woman is severely constipated or has a tendency for constipation. Picolax® may be given 24 hours prior to surgery and the woman commenced on fat-free fluids. A rectal wash-out four hours prior to surgery is then performed. In limited bowel preparation a Micralax Micro-enema® is administered two hours prior to surgery.

Neomycin 1 g and erythromycin 1 g can be given to women with gynaecological malignancies in anticipation of bowel resection. An alternative is to give IV gentamicin (120 mg) as a single bolus at the time of induction of anaesthesia. If bowel is opened during the procedure this can then be maintained (80 mg b.d.) for five days, calibrating the dose by levels at 48 hours.

Premedication

For day surgery most anaesthetists tend to avoid premedication although you should certainly discuss this with the anaesthetist concerned.

In patients having major surgery, most anaesthetists prefer to see the woman and assess the need for premedication. Premedication is by no means routine.

Drugs used for premedication are either short-acting benzodiazepines or opiates with or without droperidol. The dose of these drugs is adjusted to suit the woman according to her age and weight.

Some anaesthetists might also use additional drugs such as glyceryl trinitrite patches for patients with angina and nebulised salbutamol for patients with asthma. To avoid confusion it is advisable to ask the anaesthetist.

SCHEDULING

Ordering patients on an operating list may be a part of the resident's responsibility. It should always be done in agreement with both the consultant gynaecologist and the anaesthetist. The

Table 3.3 Assessing the risk for DVT prophylaxis		
Characteristic	**Present**	**Absent**
Age over 40 yrs		
Age over 60 yrs		
Obesity (x1.5 ideal body weight)		
Planned surgery 2 h or more		
History of DVT or PE		
Major surgery within six months		
Pregnancy		
Using an oestrogen preparation		
Immobility		
Sepsis		
Inflammatory bowel disease		
Cardiovascular disease		
Malignant disease suspected		
Previous stroke		
Known thrombophilic disorder		
Total (one point for each present risk factor)		

One risk factor or less: **LOW-RISK CATEGORY**
Two–four risk factors: **INTERMEDIATE-RISK CATEGORY**
More than four risk factors: **HIGH-RISK CATEGORY**

operating theatre will need to know well in advance the order, type and complexity of cases to enable special equipment etc. to be provided.

In units with a dedicated day-care unit there is little likelihood of having to mix inpatients with day patients. If this is not the case, then those scheduled for discharge on the day of operation should be scheduled as early as possible on the operating list. Diabetic patients should be operated on early in the day.

Women with known infected conditions, or known hepatitis carriers, should be operated on last on the list. This includes those known to be HIV positive. Theatre staff should be informed of any patients who are biohazards.

High-dependency units and intensive-care units

It is important to book admission to these units in advance. However, much will depend on local policies. If you feel that a certain patient may present significant respiratory, cardiovascular or metabolic problems following surgery, you should discuss this with your consultant and anaesthetist and make appropriate arrangements.

DOCUMENTATION

Notes should be clearly written with times and dates of all entries. If women and/or their relatives have been counselled with regard to various aspects of their problem and/or its management, this should also be recorded. Any investigations requested should be documented and when the results become available, these should be signed and filed in the patient's case notes. Anyone who is in hospital should have some note made on progress each day.

The notes are a legal record and incomplete documentation is regarded as omission, i.e. if it's not written then it was not done.

4 *Post-operative care*

It is important to understand the general response of a patient to any surgery.

1 Loss of body fluids results from:
- Loss of blood during surgery
- Surface evaporation
- Exudates into damaged tissues and wound in the immediate post-op. period

2 Lowering of plasma proteins is due to:
- Breakdown of tissue protein

3 Potassium depletion is due to:
- Increased potassium excretion by the kidneys
- Vomiting, diarrhoea, and ileus (intestinal fluids are rich in potassium)

These changes are normal physiological responses and are mediated to some extent through the stress response of the adrenal cortex. Compensation for the loss of body fluid occurs as water is taken from the extracellular space. Compensatory vasoconstriction maintains blood pressure and urine output diminishes to maintain extracellular fluid. Loss of protein is replaced by increasing the protein intake, and loss of potassium by supplements if necessary.

OTHER POST-SURGICAL PHENOMENA

In addition to the physiological responses outlined above, patients may also have:

- Pain
- Bowel dysfunction
- Bladder dysfunction
- Immobility
- Confusion and disorientation (especially in the elderly)

POST-OPERATIVE ANALGESIA

Any procedure involving an abdominal incision will cause some degree of post-operative pain. If the rectus muscles have been cut or stretched this will be more marked. Pain may also be visceral in origin, e.g. the discomfort noted by some women following tubal occlusion (tubal colic). These patients will require analgesia in varying degrees in the post-operative period.

Laparoscopy

The abdominal punctures can cause a mild degree of pain. This can be managed by either injection of a long-acting local anaesthetic at the time of surgery or, more usually, by simple oral analgesia post-operatively. Some surgeons use non-steroidal anti-inflammatory agents (NSAIDs) (e.g. Voltarol®), given rectally at completion of the operation.

Some patients may complain of shoulder-tip pain post-operatively. This is the result of diaphragmatic irritation. It passes off within 24 hours and can be managed by simple oral analgesics.

Tubal occlusion by clips or rings can also cause pain (more often with the latter). In severe cases intramuscular opiates may be required (pethidine 100 mg).

Laparotomy

Several options for pain control exist.

- The common combination of **intermittent opiate**

(morphine or papaveretum) and an anti-emetic is used far less frequently now.

- **Patient-controlled morphine** pumps provide a very satisfactory alternative with early institution of rectal non-steroidal analgesia supplemented if necessary by simple oral analgesics.

- **Epidural analgesia** also has a place in post-operative pain control using either local anaesthetics or opiates.

- Injection of **long-acting local anaesthetics** into the wound edges at the completion of surgery may also provide some pain relief.

Vaginal surgery

Vaginal surgery provokes less discomfort than abdominal procedures. Some patients may suffer from low back pain or visceral pain which usually responds to simple oral analgesia. Severe pain following vaginal procedures should arouse suspicion of pelvic haematoma or abscess.

Vulval surgery

This can cause quite severe discomfort, usually associated with bruising and oedema. Caudal analgesia (inserted at the time of surgery), rectal NSAIDs and occasionally opiates are used. Local infiltration of the operation site with 0.25% Marcaine® affords a certain degree of relief over the first 12 hours.

FLUID BALANCE

The majority of gynaecological patients will not have any associated cardiac or renal problems and will have established normal oral fluid intake within 24 hours of surgery. Ileus is uncommon following pelvic surgery. If there has been associated bowel surgery, a long anaesthetic or surgical complications, it will be necessary to maintain careful fluid balance with appropriate fluid replacement. Such patients should have an in-dwelling catheter and daily monitoring of urea and electrolytes. In cases of malignancy, especially if associated with ascites, protein replacement may need to be considered.

Where there is known cardiorespiratory compromise, or in cases requiring large volumes of fluid replacement, central venous pressure (CVP) should be monitored.

Urine output should be maintained at approximately 50 ml per hour. If this is not maintained with a rising JVP consider frusemide initially.

DIET

Patients should be encouraged to eat as soon as there is evidence of gastrointestinal activity. Fibre should be avoided initially as this may provoke cramps and colicky pain. Carbonated drinks should also be avoided in the early post-operative phase. High-protein and calorie intake in convalescence is to be encouraged.

Examples of fluid management
Routine post-operative care, first 24 hours
- 1 litre normal saline
- 2 litres 5% dextrose
- 40 mmol potassium
- Commence free fluids orally once nausea has fully subsided

Ileus anticipated or confirmed
- In-dwelling catheter
- Nasogastric suction (free drainage and four-hourly aspiration)
- 80 mmol potassium daily
- Daily urea and electrolyte measurement
- Titrate input with output
- Consider albumin in hypoproteinaemic states
- Start parenteral nutrition if >5days
- Nil by mouth, other than sips to keep mouth fresh

NAUSEA

Major pelvic surgery is often associated with more than antici-pated nausea in the post-operative phase. Some of this may be due to the use of opiate analgesics and to a certain extent can be managed by changing to non-steroidal pain relief. Inadequate pain relief in itself can lead to nausea.

It is important to consider the possibility of gastrointestinal obstruction or perforation in any woman who has undergone a pelvic operation; even a curettage where an unrecognised perfo-ration has occurred could result in bowel damage, ileus and obstruction. If on clinical assessment it is not possible to exclude this, then an IV line should be inserted, no oral intake allowed and plain X-rays of the abdomen arranged (erect and supine).

In most cases, post-operative nausea is not severe and not associated with absent or diminished bowel sounds or indeed abdominal distension. Anti-emetics such as prochlorperazine, cyclizine or metoclopramide are usually adequate.

BLADDER FUNCTION

Several gynaecological procedures may result in temporary disordered bladder function which will require catheterisation at the time of surgery. Surgery involving the bladder neck is one such example. These patients will have either suprapubic catheters or urethral catheters inserted. The former, although more difficult to insert, can be clamped to allow normal urethral voiding. The principle of post-operative bladder care is to reach the point of normal spontaneous voiding with post-void residual volumes less than 100 ml. Residual urine volumes can be easily assessed if a suprapubic catheter is *in situ*. If urethral catheters are employed, residual volume measurement will entail passing another catheter.

To improve post-operative bladder tone and encourage an early return to spontaneous voiding, catheters are usually clamped (for intervals up to four hours) to allow the bladder to fill. The clamp should be released at least four-hourly or if the woman becomes uncomfortable.

There are many varied bladder care regimens. You should find out what is the local practice. Prior to the removal of any catheter, a specimen of urine should be sent for bacteriological analysis.

SUCTION AND FREE DRAINS

Suction drains are frequently employed to minimise fluid collections in the pelvis and/or wound. They can be removed once the daily drainage rate falls below 20 ml. In certain situations they should be left in longer and only removed when dry (e.g. to reduce the risk of lymphocyst after groin node dissection for vulval cancer). Wide-bore tube and corrugated drains are usually placed when there is an infected operation site. The objective is to develop a temporary sinus to allow pus to drain freely and therefore avoid pelvic abscess formation. These drains are usually shortened gradually from the third post-operative day.

WOUND CARE

Wounds should be inspected daily and full aseptic techniques should be adhered to. Signs of erythema, warmth and swelling may indicate a wound infection or haematoma. Both can cause pyrexia but the former is likely to be more pronounced and fluctuate. Suspicion of a wound infection should prompt appropriate bacteriological investigations of any discharge. Collections of blood or pus will normally drain spontaneously, although it may be necessary to remove sutures and occasionally probe the wound to allow drainage to occur.

Wounds need only have sterile dry dressings applied after they have been inspected.

Removal of sutures and skin clips

- **Transverse abdominal wounds**
  Sutures and clips can be removed after 4–6 days.
- **Midline and paramedian incisions**
  Sutures should be left in longer (8–10 days). There is no logic in removing alternate sutures.
- **Vaginal surgery**
  Absorbable sutures are usually used. If both anterior and posterior vaginal incisions have been made, a gentle digital examination should be performed prior to the woman being discharged to prevent antero-posterior adhesion formation.

ANTI-D PROPHYLAXIS

All rhesus-negative women (who are not already sensitised) should be offered anti-D within 48 hours of:

- Threatened miscarriage
- Evacuation of retained products
- Ectopic pregnancy
- Evacuation of molar pregnancy
- Live birth or stillbirth
- Amniocentesis
- Chorion villus sampling (CVS)

POST-OPERATIVE ADVICE TO PATIENTS

Apart from the more obvious information concerning their diagnosis and further treatment, if any, women will require basic information about such things as expected level of discomfort, bladder function, sexual function and when they might expect to return to work, lift objects etc. This advice is very variable and in order to avoid any confusion should always be consistent with any information given in written information sheets or by other professionals. Some useful advice relating to common procedures and problems is given below.

Post-operative advice to patients

Dilatation and curettage
Can expect vaginal bleeding for up to a week and should not use tampons until the next period. Intercourse should be avoided for two weeks and the woman should be fit to return to work in 2–3 days.

Termination of pregnancy
As for D&C. Should be counselled with regard to contraception and the possibility of conceiving prior to next period. Can start COC, POP or depot injections on the day of, or day following, the procedure.

Miscarriage
As for D&C. Ideally should wait for at least one normal period before attempting to conceive again. If the pregnancy was unwanted the woman will need contraceptive advice. Should consider giving general preconceptual advice, e.g. using folic acid, having rubella status checked.

Ectopic pregnancy
As for miscarriage but will require GOPD review to explain risks of further ectopics and/or institute fertility management if gross tubal disease. Avoid intercourse for at least two weeks and should remain off work until OPD review. Avoid heavy lifting if woman has had a laparotomy.

Laparoscopy
Slight PV loss for 2–3 days and to avoid intercourse until bleeding has stopped. May notice some shoulder-tip discomfort. Sutures are generally absorbable; if not, district nurse should remove in three days. Woman will need 3–4 days off work.

Sterilisation
As for laparoscopy. Unless using COC continue with usual contraceptive method until next period. If using COC, continue to the end of the pack to prevent an early withdrawal bleed. If IUCD removed, use barrier methods until next period.

Bartholin's cyst or abscess
Regular baths and gentle digital insertion into cavity to keep open. No intercourse for two weeks and then to use a condom until the vaginal wall is fully healed. Sutures are absorbable.

Loop excision or laser to cervix
Bloodstained discharge for up to four weeks. If heavy with clots, the woman should contact hospital. No intercourse or tampons for four weeks. Will need follow-up smear with or without colposcopy six months after the procedure.

Hysterectomy
PV loss may persist for up to six weeks and might include some suture material. No intercourse for six weeks. To stay off work for six weeks and only start driving when she can confidently do an emergency stop. Smears will not be required if normal pre-operatively and histology benign. HRT not required if the ovaries have been conserved but should be considered in all premenopausal women (certainly under the age of 45 years) if ovaries were removed and there are no contraindications.

Pelvic-floor repairs
As for hysterectomy but will require cytology follow-up if the cervix is still *in situ*.

DISCHARGING PATIENTS

Patients should generally be considered fit for discharge when they are self-caring, mobile and tolerating a normal diet.

Disadvantages of prolonged inpatient stay
- Immobility
- Increased risk of cross-infection
- Not cost-effective
- Inconvenient for patient and relatives

The home environment should be satisfactory for safe convalescence; if necessary, additional support may be required in the home.

Important information for patients
- What the diagnosis was
- What procedures were done
- What continued therapy is necessary
- What follow-up arrangements have been made
- Young women (<50 years of age) should be counselled with regard to HRT. If they wish to have hormone replacement and there are no contraindications, then this should be prescribed
- Similarly, if there is a need for contraception, this should also be dealt with at the time of discharge

---

A brief summary of 'in-hospital' events should be written and sent at the time of discharge to the GP, together with details of any ongoing treatment and any outpatient follow-up if required.

Finally, the case notes should be checked to ensure they are complete and, if there are any outstanding results such as pathology reports, this should be noted in the case record.

Discharge checklist

- Woman medically fit for community convalescence
- Woman and GP informed of diagnosis
- Woman and GP informed of procedures
- Any drugs required prescribed
- Woman and GP aware of any discharge medication
- Any requirement for hormone replacement therapy?
- Any requirement for family planning advice?
- Satisfactory home circumstances for convalescence
- Is there a need for outpatient follow-up and if so when?
- Have both the woman and GP been informed of follow-up arrangements?
- Are any further outpatient investigations required? If so, have they been arranged?
- Case notes complete

5 Short notes on outpatient problems

These notes are not intended as a manual for outpatient practice but merely to 'point you in the right direction'. The outpatient clinic is an important area in which to learn the basic facts and clinical skills that with experience will make you a competent gynaecologist. Part of that learning process is to see and assess patients – initially supervised and eventually with less supervision.

Many problems present in the clinic. This short list takes some of the more common presentations and provides a quick resumé so that you might understand the basics. More detailed texts are certainly recommended to consolidate your background and understanding of these problems.

PELVIC MASS

A pelvic mass could represent anything from a normal pregnancy to a malignant neoplasm. The history and age of the woman will provide most of the information necessary in order to allow a management decision to be made. Having excluded pregnancy, patients should be investigated with a view to planning surgery if required. In some situations a mass may be present but the patient is asymptomatic, e.g. large fibroid. By convention, fibroids larger than approximately 12 weeks (gestation) are considered candidates for surgical management.

Conditions commonly presenting with a pelvic and/or abdominal mass are outlined in Table 5.1.

Table 5.1 Conditions commonly presenting with a pelvic and/or abdominal mass

Benign conditions	Malignant conditions
• Uterine fibroids	• Ovarian carcinoma
• Benign ovarian cysts	• Uterine sarcomas
• Endometriosis	• Bulky endometrial cancers
• Chronic inflammatory conditions (hydrosalpinx)	• Ascites and pelvic secondaries
• Pregnancy	

Table 5.2 Investigation of pelvic masses

Benign conditions	Malignant conditions
	As for benign masses plus:
Full blood count	
Biochemical profile	Tumour markers*
Mid-stream urine	Intravenous urogram
Pelvic ultrasound scan	Chest X-ray
β HCG (in possible pregnancy)	Retro-peritoneal CT scan
IVU in selected cases	Liver ultrasound scan
	Barium studies as indicated

* Tumour markers
• Serum CA 125 should be measured if ovarian cancer is suspected
• α-fetoprotein (AFP) and β HCG – in women <40 years with suspicious adnexal masses, serum AFP and β HCG should be measured. Germ cell tumours are more likely in younger women and these markers can be valuable in their assessment.

Investigation

All large and/or fixed pelvic masses should have an IVU as part of their assessment and if there is any clinical doubt with regard to whether a mass may be malignant, the investigation should be as for a high degree of suspicion of malignancy. Table 5.2 summarises the investigations that should be carried out.

Ascites

If ascites is present either clinically or on ultrasound assessment it should only be drained pre-operatively if it is causing undue discomfort or respiratory embarrassment. The tap should be placed in the midline where the needle track can be excised at laparotomy. There is a fairly frequent incidence of tumour nodules implanting at the site of ascitic drainage.

In most instances, paracentesis will confirm that there is an abdominal malignancy but will not reliably indicate the organ of origin and should be regarded as a poor substitute for histological confirmation and only contemplated if surgery is not possible.

If the ascites is loculated and/or there have been several abdominal operations it may be safer to perform the paracentesis under ultrasound guidance.

Aspirated fluid should be assessed:

- cytologically
- biochemically (for protein content)
- bacteriologically (particularly in younger women from ethnic minority groups where there is a possibility of peritoneal tuberculosis)

MENSTRUAL PROBLEMS

These represent one of the most common reasons for gynaecological referral. Both excessive blood loss at the time of menstruation (defined as >80 ml in any one period) and reduced or infrequent periods are reasons for referral. It is important to allow sufficient time to take an accurate history. What some women may describe as very frequent periods might in fact be normal periods with regular intermenstrual bleeding. Heavy and irregular bleeding is usually associated with uterine or pelvic pathology, or is classified as dysfunctional if no pathology can be demonstrated.

Amenorrhoea or oligomenorrhoea is more likely to represent ovarian dysfunction, although naturally one must exclude pregnancy in cases of amenorrhoea.

In the past, these problems were usually investigated by formal diagnostic curettage under a general anaesthetic. This procedure allowed for a thorough examination under anaesthetic and also an assessment of endometrial status. Carcinoma is very uncommon in women <40 years as are endometrial hyperplasias. Nevertheless, an endometrial sample is still indicated in these situations. These can be taken with a variety of endometrial sampling devices in an outpatient setting and do not require an anaesthetic. Pelvic ultrasound, particularly a transvaginal scan can complement an endometrial sample and together these are usually sufficient to exclude major degrees of pelvic and uterine pathology.

DYSFUNCTIONAL UTERINE BLEEDING

In the absence of organic gynaecological disease, e.g. tumour, fibroids, etc., any abnormal uterine bleeding should be regarded as being dysfunctional. This type of bleeding most commonly occurs in adolescence and premenopausally and includes all abnormal forms of menstruation except amenorrhoea.

Aetiology of dysfunctional uterine bleeding
Dysfunction in any of the following:
- Endometrium
- Ovary
- Anterior pituitary gland/hypothalamus
- Other endocrine glands, e.g. thyroid
- Haematological disorders, e.g. thrombocytopenia

Basic investigations of menstrual problems

- Full blood count
- Thyroid function (hypothyroidism can cause menorrhagia)
- Endometrial sample
- Transvaginal scan (if pelvic examination is uncertain)

Planning the management of menstrual problems

Important considerations are:

- The presumed cause of excessive bleeding (e.g. presence of fibroids)
- The woman's age and future childbearing prospects
- The woman's perception of the scale of the problem

In cases where there is obvious pelvic pathology such as fibroids or endometriosis, a surgical approach may be the correct first option. This will entail hysterectomy. In milder cases, dysfunctional bleeding may be managed by reassurance only. There are various options for medical management (see Figure 5.1). If these are to be used, it is sometimes valuable to provide a menstrual calendar so that any improvement can easily be identified. Dysfunctional bleeding that has not responded to medical management might also be managed by hysterectomy, although increasingly options such as endoscopic resection or ablation of the endometrium are being employed. These procedures are usually performed in thoroughly assessed women (to exclude malign endometrial change and gross pelvic pathology) and after preparation of the endometrium with drugs such as danazol or GnRH agonists. Both of these drugs cause thinning of the endometrium and result in an easier resection/ablation with less bleeding.

Haematological investigations are shown in Figure 5.2.

AMENORRHOEA AND OLIGOMENORRHOEA

Women presenting with infrequent or absent menstruation should be assessed slightly differently.

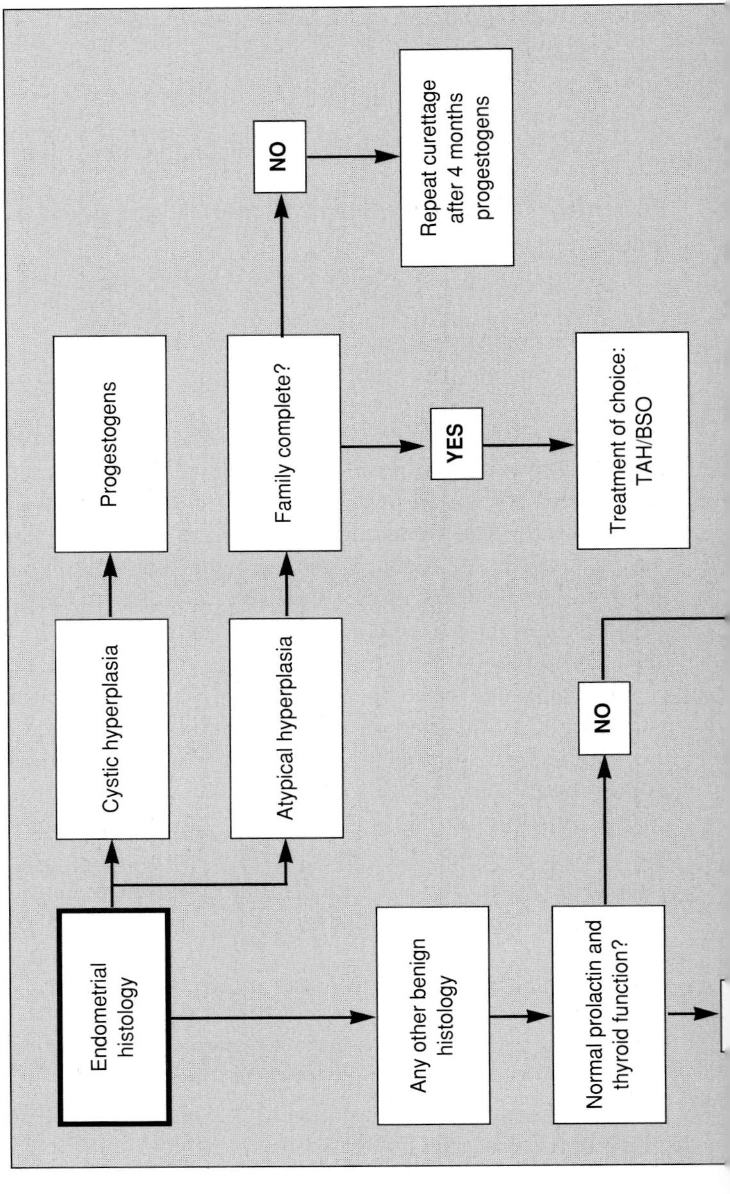

Figure 5.1 A management algorithm for dysfunctional uterine bleeding

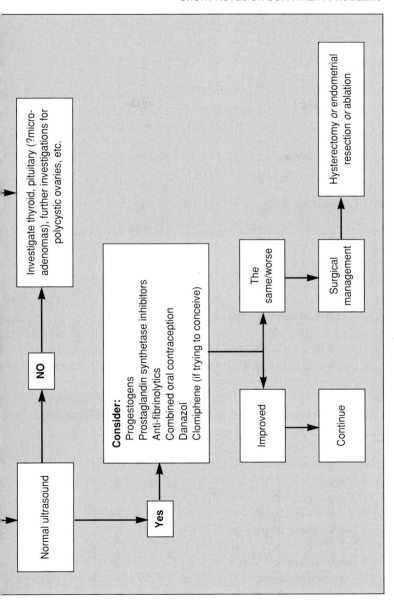

Normal ultrasound → **Yes** → **Consider:**
Progestogens
Prostaglandin synthetase inhibitors
Anti-fibrinolytics
Combined oral contraception
Danazol
Clomiphene (if trying to conceive)

Normal ultrasound → **NO** → Investigate thyroid, pituitary (?micro-adenomas), further investigations for polycystic ovaries, etc.

Improved → Continue

The same/worse → Surgical management → Hysterectomy *or* endometrial resection *or* ablation

Figure 5.2 Haematological investigations in menstrual disturbance

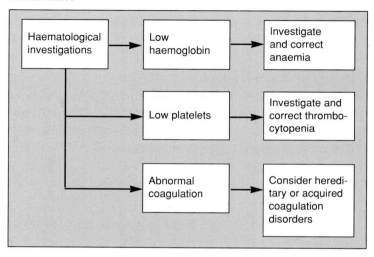

Primary amenorrhoea

In young women with primary amenorrhoea, it is important to confirm normally developed pelvic anatomy, i.e. exclude conditions such as imperforate hymen or absent uterus. Testicular feminisation and Turner's syndrome may present as a result of primary amenorrhoea and therefore if indicated by findings at clinical examination, chromosomal studies should be performed.

Causes of primary amenorrhoea
- Constitutional delayed puberty
- Pregnancy
- Primary ovarian failure
- Turner's syndrome
- Testicular feminisation
- Absent uterus
- Absent vagina
- Imperforate hymen

Investigations that might be considered in these situations include:

- Chromosomes
- Serum FSH
- Diagnostic laparoscopy

Secondary amenorrhoea

Secondary amenorrhoea should firstly arouse the possibility of pregnancy. If this can be excluded, primary ovarian failure (premature menopause), resistant ovary syndrome or polycystic ovarian disease should be considered as possibilities. In this group, systemic and general disorders, particularly weight gain and loss (anorexia), are also important to assess. Conditions such as renal failure can cause amenorrhoea, although they rarely present with this problem. It is only mentioned as correction of the underlying problem can result in resumption of ovarian activity and the subsequent risk of pregnancy.

Investigations of secondary amenorrhoea and oligomenorrhoea

- FSH and LH
- Serum androgens (including weak androgens such as androstenedione)
- Ultrasound scan for ovarian volume and morphology
- Serum oestradiol
- Thyroid function
- Serum prolactin

Young women with primary ovarian failure will require oestrogen supplementation to prevent the long-term effects of the menopause (osteoporosis, cardiovascular disease, etc.).

The management of these women will depend on the cause and their desire for future children. As long as the woman does not wish to become pregnant, if she is producing sufficient oestrogen to prevent long-term menopausal problems and if there is no evidence of underlying systemic disease, these problems require reassurance only. The women may still ovulate, albeit infrequently, and if they do not wish to become pregnant then they should be advised to use some suitable form of contraception. The pill is not contraindicated in these situations although the women should be advised that on discontinuing oral contraception they may revert to their pre-pill state.

PELVIC PAIN

This is a common cause for gynaecological referral. Pelvic pain may occur on its own, during menstruation, during intercourse, or with any combination of these.

Causes of pelvic pain
- Reproductive organs (endometriosis, pelvic infection, etc.)
- Urinary tract (urinary tract infection)
- Gastrointestinal tract (irritable bowel syndrome, diverticular disease)
- No obvious abnormality

Women who develop painful periods or dyspareunia, having previously been normal, are more likely to have developed pelvic pathology. Similarly, any abnormality noted on general and pelvic examination may also indicate pelvic disease. It can be very difficult, if not impossible, to exclude some of the common pelvic pathologies on history and examination alone. Therefore, the majority of these patients will at some stage require a laparoscopic assessment to exclude any significant pelvic disease.

Almost 50% of women complaining of pelvic pain will have no obvious abnormality on pelvic assessment and, furthermore, over 50% of this subgroup will either completely resolve or notice improvement following a negative laparoscopy. This high 'placebo response' is supportive of there being a major psychological component to the presentation. Indeed, a significant proportion of such patients do have a background of either depressive illness or significant psychosocial stress. However, it is important to assess the patient thoroughly to exclude the known pathologies. Assessment starts with a detailed history (see Table 5.3) and some valuable information can be derived by appropriate questions. It is always wise to consider a hidden agenda in these situations, e.g. marital problems, fertility problems.

Investigation

- Mid-stream urine
- Full blood count
- High vaginal and endocervical swabs (Chlamydia and gonococci)
- Pelvic ultrasound (for adnexal masses)
- Diagnostic laparoscopy

Table 5.3 Taking a history of pelvic pain

History	Possible causes
Onset of the problem	New partner – associated discharge may suggest pelvic inflammatory disease
	Following a delivery, might suggest uterine retroversion
Worse with menstruation	Possible endometriosis; PID
Associated infertility	Possible endometriosis or PID
Painful intercourse	Retroversion, PID or endometriosis
Constipation, diarrhoea or both	Irritable bowel syndrome
Intermittent or colicky	Possible torsion of an ovarian cyst
Irregular and heavy periods	Associated pelvic infection
Problem deteriorating	More likely to represent pathology
Cyclical and mid-cycle	Possible ovulation pain

Pelvic congestion

In some women with essentially normal laparoscopies (i.e. no endometriosis, PID adhesions), grossly dilated broad ligament and mesovarian veins can be seen. This situation has been described as pelvic congestion syndrome and ideally requires venography to demonstrate excessive dilatation of the pelvic veins. However, the frequency with which pelvic venous congestion occurs in asymptomatic women remains unknown, thus the significance of such findings is still uncertain.

VAGINAL DISCHARGE

Discharge from the vagina may be associated with vaginitis (trichomonas, candida, gardnerella), neoplasms, ectropion or may be physiological. Women in the reproductive phase have a normal mucous discharge from the cervix that increases in wateriness at the time of ovulation. Mucus is often described as white (as it becomes white when it dries) and is virtually never irritant. Candidiasis causes itching and is associated with a heavy white cottage-cheese-like discharge. Trichomonas causes a watery, offensive-smelling green discharge. Chlamydial and gonococcal infections also produce discharges but as a result of cervicitis, not vaginitis, and therefore an endocervical swab is required. Enquiry regarding the partner should be part of the history. Children and postmenopausal women may also develop vaginal discharges and these are usually due to atrophic vaginitis and infection with non-specific pathogens. Children might also have a discharge due to a foreign body.

Investigation

In adults

- Vulval and vaginal inspection
- Cervical inspection and smear
- High vaginal swab
- Endocervical swab
- Urethral, rectal and pharyngeal swabs if gonococci suspected

- Wet preparation of vaginal secretions
- Amine test for gardnerella (bacterial vaginosis)

In children

This should not be delegated to a junior gynaecologist as there is the possibility of sexual abuse and nearly always the fear that the child has been abused (as far as the parents are concerned). In most situations the child will be best examined under a general anaesthetic as this will be far more revealing and allow for bacteriological specimens to be taken. Scratch marks around the vulva are not unusual but tears or scarring may well indicate abuse. The perineum, anus and anal canal should also be inspected for signs of trauma and infestation.

NOTES ON VAGINAL DISCHARGE

- Specific infections should be treated with the appropriate antibiotic or fungicide and the partner should also be treated.
- Contact tracing is appropriate in cases of chlamydia and gonococci.
- Sexually transmitted diseases, not uncommonly, are present as multiple infections.
- Candidiasis is not regarded as a sexually transmitted disease although it can be spread to partners.
- Discharge due to cervical ectropion can be treated by Aci-Jel® but if this is not effective in bringing about squamous metaplasia then treatment should be by cautery to the exposed cervical glandular epithelium (cryocautery, cold coagulation or diathermy).
- It is important to have evidence of a recent negative cervical smear prior to performing cautery.
- Physiological discharges require a careful explanation and reassurance that no infection is present. Even if the woman is fully counselled that no infection is present a minority will continue to seek medical advice regarding their discharge.

ENDOMETRIOSIS

The definition of endometriosis is the presence of endometrial deposits outside the uterus in ectopic sites. These deposits are dependent on ovarian hormones for their survival. Table 5.4 lists the sites for endometriosis.

Symptoms

The symptoms (see Table 5.5) are largely dependent upon which structures are involved but it is important to note that the severity of symptoms need not reflect the extent of disease, i.e. a small amount of endometriosis may be associated with quite severe dysmenorrhoea whilst extensive pelvic disease can be asymptomatic.

Treatment

The medical treatment of endometriosis is shown in Table 5.6.

Management of endometriosis

Management will depend on:
- the symptoms and extent of disease
- the woman's age and desire to retain her fertility
- whether infertility is a presenting problem.

The management is summarised in Figures 5.3 and 5.4.

HRT after TAH and BSO for endometriosis

Following removal of the uterus and ovaries, women may require hormone replacement therapy. This is not contraindicated in women who have been diagnosed as having endometriosis. There are no substantive data suggesting that this will lead to reactivation of endometriosis, although there have been some sporadic case reports of this occurring.

Table 5.4 Sites for endometriosis

Common	Less common
Ovary	Umbilicus
Uterus	Previous scar from abdominal operation
Pelvic and abdominal peritoneum	Bowel
Round and uterosacral ligaments	Lungs
Fallopian tubes	Bladder
Rectovaginal septum	

Table 5.5 Symptoms and signs of endometriosis

Symptoms:

Pain
- Dysmenorrhoea
- Premenstrual pain
- Deep dyspareunia
- Painful scars (abdominal, episiotomy etc.)

Menstruation
- Menorrhagia
- Irregular bleeding

Uncommon symptoms include:
Symptoms associated with intestinal obstruction, rectal bleeding, haemoptysis and/or pleuritic pain at the time of menstruation.

Signs:
- Uterus may be uniformly enlarged/tender
- Uterus may be retroverted/fixed
- Adnexal enlargement/swelling – 'chocolate' cysts/tender
- Tender nodules in pouch of Douglas/vaginal vault
- Rarely there may be signs and symptoms of intestinal obstruction
- Endometriotic nodules/swelling in previous operation scar

Table 5.6 Medical treatment of endometriosis

Choice of drug	Dosage	Contraindications	Side-effects
OC pill		Pregnancy; thrombosis; liver disease; breast and endometrial cancer; migraine (see *BNF* for complete list)	Nausea; vomiting; headache breast tenderness; weight gain; depression; thrombo-embolism; hypertension; impaired liver function
Progestogens			
Dydrogesterone	10–30 mg daily	High-risk groups; liver disease; jaundice; severe arterial disease	Acne; weight gain (fluid retention); breast discomfort urticaria; change in libido; nausea
Norethisterone	10–25 mg daily		
Medroxyproge-sterone acetate	30 mg daily		
Natural progesterone			
Pessaries (Cyclogest®)	400 mg b.d.		
Danol®	400–800 mg daily	Liver disease; cardiac/renal impairment; thrombo-embolic disease	Nausea; dizziness; rashes; weight gain and flushes; musculo-skeletal pain; reduction in breast size; hair loss; acne; clitoromegaly
Gestrinone	2.5 µg x 2 per week	As for Danol®	As for Danol®
GnRH agonists			
Nafarelin (nasal spray)	200 µg b.d.	Pregnancy or breast feeding	Hot flushes; vaginal dryness; change in libido; decrease in breast size; headaches; irritation of nasal passages; calcium loss from bones
Buserelin (nasal spray)	100 µg 4–5 times daily	As above	As above
Goserelin (depot injection into abdominal wall)	3.6 mg per month (s.c.)	As above	As above but no nasal irritation

Figure 5.3 Management of endometriosis in young women or those wishing to retain their fertility

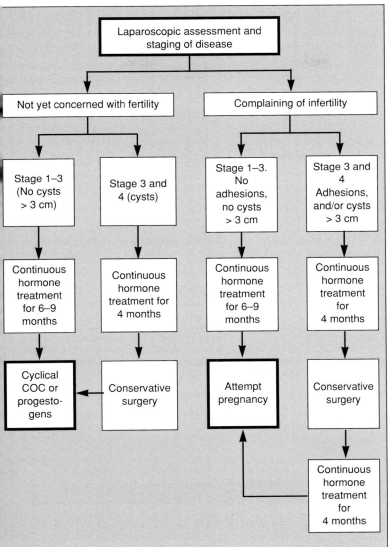

Figure 5.4 Management of endometriosis in older women or those not wishing to retain their fertility

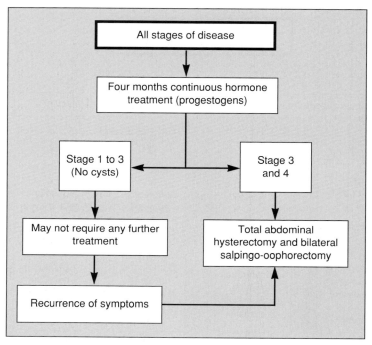

BLADDER PROBLEMS

The most common problems relating to micturition are:
- Urinary incontinence
- Urinary frequency
- Dysuria
- Urgency

URINARY INCONTINENCE

Genuine stress incontinence

No abnormality of detrusor function, incontinence resulting

from a weakness or deficiency in the urethral 'valvular' mechanism. These patients classically give a history of passing small amounts of urine only at times of rapid increases in intra-abdominal pressure such as occurs when coughing, laughing or occasionally on exercising. On examination, incontinence can usually be demonstrated when the woman is asked to strain. There may also be an associated cystocoele or significant laxity of the anterior vaginal wall. Supporting the urethrovesical angle with the examining finger will often result in abolition of incontinence when the woman strains.

Urge incontinence

Usually associated with detrusor instability. This may be a temporary phenomenon associated with a urinary tract infection or may be the result of more permanent detrusor dysfunction. The two types of incontinence often co-exist.

A thorough history and examination is required with particular reference to fluid intake and output patterns. Examination should be aimed at detecting any abnormalities of vaginal anatomy and the possible presence of pelvic masses. Factors that might exacerbate stress incontinence, such as obesity, chronic chest infection, etc., should be documented. The presence or absence of other hernias that might indicate a genetic predisposition to weak collagen and thus prolapse should also be noted. If major degrees of uterovaginal prolapse are present, the possibility of incomplete bladder emptying and occasionally ureteric reflux should be considered.

Initial investigation of urinary incontinence

- Mid-stream urine for culture and sensitivity
- Biochemical profile for assessment of renal function
- Basic urodynamic assessment (cystometry and urethral pressure profile)

Management of incontinence

- **Genuine stress incontinence** is best managed surgically although physiotherapy can bring about substantial improvements in some patients. Fitting a vaginal ring pessary is a useful temporary measure and may be a permanent option in the very frail woman.
- **Urge incontinence** is primarily managed medically (anticholinergics). Careful attention to fluid intake, bladder retraining and drugs such as oxybutinin (up to 20 mg daily in divided doses; in the elderly start at 5 mg daily and increase slowly) can be of value.

PROLAPSE

This occurs as a result of the pelvic floor ligaments and musculature failing to support either the bladder (cystocoele), uterus (uterovaginal prolapse and procidentia), pouch of Douglas (enterocoele) or rectum (rectocoele). Presentation is usually by a sensation of 'something coming down', there may also be an associated deep dragging pain referred to the lower back. There may be disturbed bladder or bowel function as a consequence of the anatomical changes brought about by the prolapse.

Factors predisposing to prolapse
- Childbirth (particularly large babies or prolonged labours)
- The menopause
- Previous pelvic surgery (hysterectomy)
- Chronic increased intra-abdominal pressure (masses, constipation, chronic cough)
- Inherited collagen weakness (Ehlers-Danlos syndrome)

Symptoms and signs of prolapse

Women may complain of a sensation of 'something coming down'. This may be the only presenting symptom. Other symptoms that may be present include:

- Urinary incontinence (usually associated with a cystocoele)
- Dragging pelvic and low back pain (worse after prolonged standing and relieved by lying down)
- A lump appearing at the introitus (cystocoele, rectocoele or procidentia)
- Difficulty with defaecation (has to replace the lump into the vagina to empty bowels)

If a prolapse has remained outside the vagina for any length of time it may become roughened, hyperkeratotic or even ulcerated as a result of drying of the vaginal epithelium and chronic irritation from underclothes.

Management

These contributory factors will direct the initial assessment and if any aggravating factors are found such as constipation or chronic cough, these should be dealt with first. The type, site and extent of prolapse should be documented along with the woman's future fertility plans (if appropriate) and her current sexual activity status.

Conservative approaches to management include pelvic floor physiotherapy, and the insertion of inert vaginal pessaries (usually soft rubber ring pessaries). These forms of management are appropriate in those too frail to undergo surgery or who are contemplating further pregnancies in the near future. They are also valuable approaches to use in women awaiting a surgical repair.

Surgery must take account of future fertility, sexual activity, the type and degree of prolapse and whether or not there is an associated dysfunction of the bladder and/or bowel.

In some women who might be unsuitable for general anaesthesia but who would benefit from surgical correction, a repair under epidural or spinal analgesia can be performed.

FAMILY PLANNING

Women using combined oral contraception (COC) should discontinue at least one month prior to major surgery. They should be advised to use barrier methods in the interim.

Women having major surgery need not have intrauterine devices removed prior to surgery – the devices can be removed after the women have been anaesthetised.

Women who remain fertile after their operative procedures, and especially those who have had terminations of pregnancy, should be offered family-planning advice prior to discharge from hospital.

Methods of family planning
- Combined oral contraception
- Postcoital contraception
- Progestogen-only contraception
- Injectable progestogen
- Intrauterine device
- Sterilisation
- Barrier method and spermicide

Combined oral contraception (COC)

There are many different brands available. All contain an oestrogen (usually ethinyl oestradiol) and a progestogen (levonorgestrel, norethisterone, gestodene, desogestrel). Most COCs contain 30 µg of oestrogen. Higher dose pills (50 µg) are useful in the management of some menstrual disorders. Pills containing third-generation progestogens (gestodene, desogestrel) have minimal effects, if any, on the lipid profile and should be regarded as first choice.

Some pills are triphasic, i.e. the content of pills change as the cycle progresses. Age alone is not a contraindication to using the COC. Advancing age, obesity, hypertension, family history of stroke and heart disease and smoking are all *relative* contraindications to COC use, not absolute.

Starting the COC

In women who have had either a miscarriage or therapeutic termination, the pill can be started straight away. Additional precautions, i.e. barrier methods, should be used for the first cycle.

The pill can be started on day one or day five of the normal cycle. If the latter is chosen, then additional precautions are advised for the first 14 days.

Factors affecting efficacy of COC

- **Other drugs are ingested:**
  Antibiotics
  Anticonvulsants
- **Gastro-intestinal disturbance**
  Vomiting
  Diarrhoea

Postcoital contraception

There are two approaches to this problem:

1 $2 \times 50\,\mu g$ COCs 12-hourly
   - The usual dosage is $100\,\mu g$ of ethinyloestradiol and $500\,\mu g$ of levonorgestrel (equal to 2 tablets of Ovran®), repeated after 12 hours.
   - Must be taken within 48 hours of unprotected intercourse
   - Not 100% effective
   - Can cause nausea and/or vomiting
2 Fitting an IUCD
   - Effective up to seven days following unprotected sexual intercourse
   - Not 100% effective
   - Skill required to fit

If vomiting occurs, a further dose should be taken or an intrauterine device fitted. A barrier method should be used until the next period. Follow-up to discuss future contraception is important.

Progestogen-only contraception (POP)

The main indication for the POP is when the COC pill is contraindicated, such as in the older woman who smokes. It is also used during lactation as it does not inhibit lactation.

The main problems are related to side-effects, such as irregular bleeding. There is also a very small increased risk of ectopic pregnancy. It should not be given to women with trophoblastic disease till HCG levels are undetectable.

The POP should be taken every day and within three hours of the same time each day, and should be started on the first day of the cycle.

Injectable progestogen

The two depot progestogens in use are medroxyprogesterone acetate (Depo-Provera®) 150 mg, given every 12 weeks, and norethisterone enanthate (NEN ET), given every eight weeks.

Both are given by a deep intramuscular injection in the first five days of the cycle. The injection site should not be rubbed, as this might cause release of the hormone. If given in the puerperium, it should be given about five weeks after delivery.

Ovulation is inhibited, compliance is not a problem and the method is reversible. The median delay to the return of fertility is about six months. It is the method of choice for patients with sickle cell disease as it reduces the number of crisis attacks.

The commonest side-effect is menstrual irregularity. Other problems may be weight gain or depression. There no increased risk of ectopic pregnancy.

Intrauterine contraceptive device (IUCD)

Commonly used IUCDs are Gravigard®, Multiload® and Ortho Gyne-T®. They are all designed to fit the contour of the uterus and prevent expulsion, whilst minimising the risk of perforation.

The IUCD is inserted either towards the end of a period or at mid-cycle. Following insertion, the woman should be told to use a barrier method of contraception for the next six weeks, at which time she should be re-examined to ensure that the threads indicate the IUCD to be in the correct position. If the threads cannot be seen, then either the IUCD has been expelled or it has been drawn up into the uterine cavity or even perforated through the uterus into the peritoneal cavity. Before performing any uterine procedure, pregnancy should always be excluded.

IUCDs, especially the newer ones, do not need replacing more often than every five years. The Multiload® Cu 375 is effective for at least eight years. A device fitted in a woman aged 40 or above does not need to be refitted.

The most recent type of IUCD is one which releases progestogen directly into the uterine cavity. This device releases 20 µg levonorgestrel per 24 hours and is effective for three years. The device has an effect of either reducing or abolishing the amount of menstrual loss and may be particularly suitable for women who wish to use an IUCD yet who have heavy periods.

Contraindications for IUCD use
See Table 5.7.

Table 5.7 Contraindications for IUCD use	
Absolute contraindications	**Relative contraindications**
Active pelvic infection	Nulliparity
Recent STD (within 12 months)	Small uterus
Genital tract bleeding of unknown cause	Distorted uterus (fibroids; congenital malformations)
Copper allergy*	Bacteraemic risk**
Wilson's disease*	

* Copper-containing devices
** Valvular heart disease, immunosuppressed patients

Problems with IUCDs
- Heavy menstruation
- Dysmenorrhoea
- Pelvic sepsis
- Ectopic gestation*
- Perforation at fitting

*IUCDs are better at preventing intrauterine pregnancies than ectopic pregnancies. There is, however, no convincing evidence that the IUCD causes ectopic pregnancy.

Sterilisation

In the UK, the number of couples seeking permanent contraception has increased as concern is expressed about efficacy and safety of other methods of contraception. Careful counselling is required. It is important for the couple to realise that it is a permanent and irreversible form of contraception. Paradoxically, there is a failure rate associated with most forms of sterilisation, and the couples should be aware of this also. They should realise that fertility only, and not sexuality, will be affected. The two main forms of sterilisation are vasectomy and tubal occlusion.

Barrier methods and spermicidal creams/gels

The condom and diaphragm are still relatively popular methods of family planning and have the added benefit of providing some protection from sexually transmitted diseases (especially condoms). They are wholly dependent on being used appropriately and efficiently. Diaphragms require fitting to ensure proper occlusion of the cervix and the woman will need to be taught how to insert the device.

The device should be inserted prior to intercourse after applying a spermicide to the cervical aspect of the device. It should remain in place for at least six hours following intercourse.

Women who require a diaphragm fitting following childbirth should be kept on follow-up until involution is complete, as there will be a need to resize and refit the device as the pelvic organs decrease in size.

INFERTILITY

One in five couples will find difficulty in conceiving therefore requests for infertility investigations are commonly seen in gynaecological clinics. Investigations usually commence after 12 months' unprotected intercourse has failed to result in conception. In some situations it is wise to institute investigations earlier, particularly if there is an apparent cause, i.e. previously confirmed pelvic inflammatory disease or a history of orchitis.

This type of problem relates to couples and ideally the history and examination should include both partners. It is important to determine if either partner has previously demonstrated that they are fertile.

Direction of the history and examination for infertility

- Past history of both partners, i.e. testicular infection or trauma, pelvic inflammatory disease
- Is normal intercourse taking place?
- The frequency and timing of intercourse
- Are sufficient, mobile, normal sperms present?
- Is the cycle regular?
- Any previous cycle irregularity
- Any symptomatic suggestion of ovulation, i.e. midcycle pain, discharge
- Any galactorrhoea or drug history that may cause hyperprolactinaemia
- Are the fallopian tubes patent and normal?
- Any antisperm antibodies

Basic investigations

- Rubella immune status
- Seminal fluid analysis
- Serum progesterone on day 21 of a 28-day cycle or seven days prior to expected menstruation
- Serum prolactin
- Diagnostic laparoscopy and tubal patency test (once normal seminal fluid analysis available)

More specialised investigations and interventions should ideally be conducted in designated infertility clinics.

THE MENOPAUSE

Most women with menopausal problems will be seen, assessed and managed by their general practitioners. Some, however, are referred for a gynaecological opinion.

Definition

The menopause is usually defined as a period of 12 months' amenorrhoea. Of course, many women will have symptoms and signs suggestive of the menopause yet not fit into this category.

Symptoms of the menopause

Classical symptoms
- Vasomotor disturbance (hot flushes and night sweats)
- Vaginal dryness (causing dyspareunia)
- Loss of libido

Other symptoms*
- Mood swings
- Irritability
- Tiredness
- Depression

* These are probably secondary to sleep disturbance associated with frequent night sweats.

The psychological problems may be considerable and relate to the woman's feelings of loss (no longer able to reproduce) and declining femininity (loss of attractiveness). Most women will enter the menopause naturally and not have severe symptoms. Some, however, will have lost their ovarian function at a young age (surgical removal of the ovaries and premature menopause).

Diagnosis

If the diagnosis is in doubt serum gonadotrophins and serum oestradiol can be measured. Raised gonadotrophins and a low oestradiol confirm ovarian failure.

Management

After a full explanation of this physiological state some women are reassured and require no treatment. In others hormone replacement therapy (HRT) may be required.

Indications for HRT

- Symptoms that the woman wishes treatment for having been fully counselled with regard to the risks and side-effects of HRT (see below)
- Surgical castration at a young age
- Increased risk of osteoporosis or cardiovascular disease

The risks associated with HRT

These are few. One of the major concerns is the relationship with breast cancer. At present few women with breast cancer receive HRT although the evidence supporting a direct association of HRT with increased relapse or progression of cancer is certainly not robust. Women with a family history of breast cancer also pose problems as it is not known if taking HRT will increase the risk further in women already thought to be at risk. There are some data suggesting a small increase in the risk of developing breast cancer in women taking HRT. This risk is, by and large, well offset by the potential advantages to the woman. Regular mammography should certainly be offered to women who might be at increased risk and also probably to most women using HRT.

Hypertension is not a contraindication to using HRT. In some women, improved blood pressure control is noted once HRT is commenced. It is wise to control the hypertension first (if indicated) and to monitor the blood pressure regularly. Cerebrovascular accident is one of the adverse outcomes of hypertension. Oestrogen-only HRT is known to improve the lipid profile and may therefore reduce the risk of stroke in some individuals.

HRT with an intact uterus
Women who have the uterus *in situ* will require progestogens in addition to oestrogen to reduce the risk of endometrial hyperplasia and neoplasia.

Administration of HRT
- Orally (daily)
- Transdermal route (patches applied twice per week, gels massaged in daily)
- Implant: implants (50 or 100 mg oestradiol) are inserted under a local anaesthetic and are usually replaced every six months
- Local vaginal oestrogen (creams or oestrogen-containing rings)

Women with intact uteri still require cyclical progestogens when using implants. In some women a condition called tachyphylaxis occurs. They find that their menopausal symptoms start to recur at shorter intervals and if the serum oestradiol is measured it is found to be in the supraphysiological range. Ideally, an attempt should be made to reduce the dose of oestrogen gradually, although this can be difficult, particularly if their symptoms are debilitating.

Any woman with an intact uterus who has unscheduled bleeding whilst using HRT requires an endometrial assessment.

CERVICAL SMEARS

A screening policy exists with regard to cervical smears. Women between the ages of 20 and 65 are offered regular smear tests, usually by their general practitioners, on a 3–5–yearly basis. If a woman has had an abnormal smear, her name will usually have been removed from the recall register and will be held on a suspended list until the appropriate action and follow-up has been completed. More women seen in gynaecology departments will now have been included in the screening programme and *ad hoc* cervical smears taken either on admission or in the clinic are to be discouraged.

Indications for taking cervical smears

- Last smear abnormal and repeat recommended
- No recorded smear in the preceding three years
- Clinical examination reveals a suspicious cervix

Assessment prior to hysterectomy

Smear status should always be checked in all women having hysterectomies and if not done should be done and the result available prior to surgery. If the smear is abnormal, colposcopy should be arranged prior to surgery to accurately define the ecto-cervical limit of the transformation zone. This precaution will minimise the risk of leaving malign epithelium sequestered at the vaginal vault (post-hysterectomy VaIN).

Interpretation of cervical smear reports and management of abnormal smears are shown in Tables 5.8 and 5.9.

TROPHOBLASTIC DISEASE

Trophoblastic disease is a pregnancy-related complication and can be divided into:

- Complete hydatidiform mole
- Partial hydatidiform mole

- Invasive hydatidiform mole
- Choriocarcinoma

The incidence of hydatidiform mole varies according to race; e.g. the incidence is less than one in 1000 pregnancies in the continental US, whereas in Japan the incidence is doubled.

Table 5.8 Interpreting cervical smear reports

Report	Explanation
Negative	A normal smear
Borderline	Minor changes, not severe enough to be termed dyskaryosis
Mild dyskaryosis	Cells compatible with but not diagnostic of CIN 1
Moderate dyskaryosis	Cells compatible with but not diagnostic of CIN 2
Severe dyskaryosis	Cells compatible with but not diagnostic of CIN 3
? Invasion	There is a possibility that invasive disease is present
Unsatisfactory	Insufficient cells or badly prepared slide
Additional comments seen on smear reports	
Koilocytes	Cytological features suggestive of human papillomavirus
Actinomycetes	Infection seen in some IUCD users
Endometrial cells	Cells from the uterine cavity
Malignant glandular cells	Cells suggestive of adenocarcinoma or adenocarcinoma-in-situ
Infecting agents (herpes, candida, trichomonas, etc.)	Indicating an ongoing infection with specified agent
No endocervical or metaplastic cells	The cervical transformation zone may not have been sampled

Table 5.9   Management of abnormal smears

Report	Management
Borderline nuclear abnormalities	If this is the first abnormal smear, repeat in six months; if not, requires colposcopy
Mild dyskaryosis	If this is the first abnormal smear, repeat in six months; if not, requires colposcopy
Moderate and severe dyskaryosis	Refer for colposcopy
Possible invasion	Urgent colposcopy
Unsatisfactory	Repeat in three months
Specific infectious agent	Treat appropriately and repeat smear (three months) if not negative
Any cytological abnormality in a previously treated woman	Refer for colposcopy

Choriocarcinoma is uncommon in the US (one per 24,000–70,000 pregnancies), but may be as frequent as one in 500–3000 in South East Asia.

Various risk factors in addition to race have been noted and Table 5.10 shows the factors that appear to be common to both hydatidiform mole and choriocarcinoma.

Table 5.10   Factors predisposing to trophoblastic disease

- Previous molar pregnancy
- Maternal age >40 years
- Teenage pregnancy
- Blood group A women with blood group O consorts

Clinical features

- Signs and symptoms of pregnancy – amenorrhoea, and occasional vaginal bleeding together with a brownish discharge. Vesicles may also be passed *per vaginam*
- Nausea and vomiting may be excessive
- Uterus may appear larger than dates
- Absence of fetal heart
- May be signs of pre-eclampsia
- May be signs of thyrotoxicosis

Diagnosis

- Due to excessive quantities of HCG being produced the urine pregnancy tests are usually positive in dilution.
- Appearances of vesicles in vaginal discharge.
- Ultrasound – absence of fetus and characteristic 'snow storm' appearance of placental tissue. Theca lutein cysts may also be seen.

Investigations

- FBC and platelets
- Group and save serum
- Chest X-ray
- Liver function tests
- Thyroid function tests
- Serum β HCG
- CSF β HCG if CNS involvement suspected
- Liver USS if hepatic metastases suspected

Management

- Suction curettage
- Prostaglandin (extra-amniotic) and syntocinon
- Hysterectomy

Suction curettage is usually the method of choice. Hysterectomy may be considered, however, in the older woman who has no desire for further children and is seeking sterilisation.

Hysterectomy may, however, be necessary if complications occur, e.g. haemorrhage/perforation of uterus.

Complications of hydatidiform mole
- Haemorrhage
- Perforation of uterus
- Sepsis
- Rupture of theca lutein cysts
- Rarely, disseminated intravascular coagulation (DIC) can occur
- Adult respiratory distress syndrome (ARDS)
- Molar metastases
- Choriocarcinoma

Follow-up

Choriocarcinoma or persistent mole is much more likely to occur following a hydatidiform mole and these women require careful follow-up. Follow-up is based on urinary β HCG measurement and is usually conducted through one of three supra-regional centres (Dundee, Sheffield and Charing Cross Hospital, London).

- Serial measurement of HCG (weekly initially to ensure levels falling) – levels should be normal after eight weeks.
- Registration for follow-up at one of three reference laboratories: Dundee, Sheffield or Charing Cross Hospital in London.
- Further bleeding warrants another ultrasound scan and a repeat evacuation of the uterus.
- Approximately 7–8% of patients will need chemotherapy if the mole does not regress.
- Women should be told to avoid pregnancy for one year.
- When HCG levels have returned to normal oral contraception may be taken.
- In subsequent pregnancies it is important to monitor HCG levels six and 12 weeks after delivery in view of the increased risk of molar pregnancy in these women.

In women who develop choriocarcinoma, 50% of the antecedent pregnancies will be molar pregnancies. In the remainder, the preceding pregnancy will have been a normal pregnancy, an abortion or an ectopic pregnancy. It is beyond the scope of this book to discuss the management of persistent hydatidiform mole or choriocarcinoma in any great degree. The mainstay of treatment, however, is with the cytotoxic agents methotrexate/folinic acid, whilst etoposide and actinomycin D and vincristine can also be used.

6 *Minor gynaecological procedures*

TAKING A CERVICAL SMEAR

When to take a smear

Smears should not be taken if the woman is menstruating as the menstrual blood may obscure the cytological pattern. As there is a UK National Screening programme, *ad hoc* smears should only be taken if the cervix is clinically suspicious or the woman has symptoms suggestive of malignancy. Antenatal smears are still taken but this time and the immediate postnatal period should ideally be avoided as again the samples are poorer and, particularly in the antenatal period, the error rate is higher as there is a general reluctance to scrape the cervix firmly.

Approximately 10–15% of the smears are unsatisfactory samples and have to be repeated; this is usually because they contain too few or poorly preserved cells.

Where to take a smear from

Samples should be taken from the squamocolumnar junction which is easily recognised as the zone between the glandular epithelium of the endocervical canal and the native squamous epithelium that covers the ectocervix. Dysplastic change originates in this zone where metaplastic change is normal. If the woman has had a hysterectomy and a vaginal vault smear is required, this should be taken from the area of the vault scar and the angles at either extent of the scar.

Situations where a cervical smear should be taken

- No record of a previous smear in any woman with a cervix aged between 20 and 65 years
- No record of a previous smear within the last three years* in any woman with a cervix aged between 23 and 65 years
- Clinically suspicious cervix
- Symptoms possibly suggesting malignancy (PCB)
- Six months following a first borderline or mildly dyskaryotic smear
- No record of normal cytology prior to planned hysterectomy
- Six months after treatment for CIN
- Vaginal vault smears should be taken six and 18 months after hysterectomy if an abnormal smear was present prior to hysterectomy and/or CIN was found at hysterectomy

*The national call and recall programme recommends that a smear should be repeated at intervals of 3–5 years.

Taking the smear

The woman should be in the dorsal or left-lateral position.

Under good light insert a bivalve speculum with minimal lubrication and expose the cervix. Any light bloodstaining or discharge seen should be gently swabbed clear with cotton wool. The characteristics of the cervix should be noted, i.e. the presence or absence of ectropion, polyps, etc., or if there is a clinical suspicion of malignancy.

Various types of wooden or plastic spatulae or brushes have been recommended for collecting the sample. The most commonly used are the wooden Ayres and Aylesbury spatulae. The choice of spatula is of less importance than the skill of the smear taker. The spatula is applied to the external os so as to sweep the area where the squamocolumnar junction is sited. It is then rotated through 360° in one direction then the process is reversed, sweeping in the other direction. Relatively firm pressure should be applied.

The scrapings are then spread evenly (in a linear not circular manner) along a prepared and identified (with name and number) glass slide. The sample should be fixed immediately, either by spraying with or immersing in a suitable fixative. This should then be sent off to the cytology laboratory with a properly completed request form.

Taking an adequate smear often provokes some bleeding. This should be explained to the patient and she should be reassured that the bleeding will stop within 24 hours.

Having taken a smear it is important to:

- Ensure that you are aware of the result
- Set in motion appropriate action
- Inform the patient of the result and the action. *After having a smear taken, women should be informed what will happen if the test is normal and what will happen if the test is not normal.*

REMOVAL OF CERVICAL POLYPS

Cervical polyps are not uncommon. They are usually asymptomatic and found at examinations, usually at the time a cervical smear is taken. The vast majority are benign and are based on narrow stalks. These can be quite easily, and painlessly avulsed without recourse to anaesthesia. Large vascular or broad-based polyps are best managed under general anaesthetic.

Having exposed the cervix and gently swabbed the ectocervix with a mild antiseptic solution, the polyp should be grasped with polyp forceps. The forceps are then locked and rotated. Continue rotation until the stalk is avulsed and the polyp comes away. The polyp should be sent for histological assessment. If there is any bleeding, the base of the stalk can be cauterised by applying either silver nitrate or Monsell's solution (paste). Follow-up is not required unless the histology of the polyp necessitates further action.

In women complaining of menstrual disturbance or post-menopausal bleeding, the presence of a polyp cannot be assumed to be the cause of the bleeding. These women will require further investigation directed at excluding endometrial pathology.

ENDOMETRIAL SAMPLING

This is an outpatient technique and the objective is to achieve a representative sample of endometrial tissue for histological assessment. Cases such as suspected dysfunctional uterine bleeding, postmenopausal bleeding or postcoital bleeding might often be assessed in this way. If no tissue is retrieved and the presenting problem persists, a more formal curettage under a general anaesthetic will be required to exclude the possibility of having missed endometrial pathology.

Endometrial sampling does not require cervical dilatation and a number of different implements have been developed to sample the endometrium. Before taking a sample, a bimanual examination should be performed to assess the size, position and mobility of the uterus and also to assess the adnexae. If a cervical smear is also required, this should be performed first.

A bivalve speculum is inserted to adequately expose the cervix which is best stabilised by grasping the anterior lip with a volsellum. This might cause some discomfort. Having stabilised and swabbed the cervix with an aqueous hibitane solution, an appropriate endometrial sampling device is gently inserted into the cervical canal and advanced so that the sampling tip lies in the endometrial cavity. If the device will not pass through the canal with gentle forward pressure, the procedure should be abandoned as forcible dilatation of the cervix causes pain and may bring about a vasovagal collapse.

A representative sample is collected by rotating the device to collect tissue from all of the endometrial cavity surfaces

CHANGING A RING PESSARY

The woman should be asked whether or not the ring is causing any problems, e.g. discomfort, bleeding or discharge. If so, the size of the ring may need changing or further investigations may be required for bleeding or discharge.

Removing a ring pessary

Using a gloved hand and K-Y Jelly®, the index finger and thumb of the right hand are inserted into the vagina and the anterior portion of the ring which is lying behind the symphysis pubis is grasped and the ring is rotated through 90° whilst traction is applied in a downwards direction to effect removal of the ring.

A Cusco's speculum is inserted and the general condition of the vaginal vault is noted, with particular attention being paid to the size of any vaginal vault prolapse and the condition of the vaginal mucosa. If any ulcerations are noted the ring should not be reinserted and advice should be sought from a senior colleague. If any vaginal discharge is present a swab should be taken for microbiological examination.

Refitting a ring pessary

The old ring should be thoroughly washed, dried and coated in Dienoestrol cream. The labia are then parted with the left hand, the ring is grasped in the right hand and squeezed to form a narrow oval shape, and gently reinserted into the vagina in the sagittal plane. The ring is gently rotated through 90° in a clockwise direction as it is inserted into the vagina. The most posterior part of the ring should lie in the posterior fornix and the anterior part should be lying immediately behind and above the symphysis pubis. The cervix should be palpable within the central deficit of the ring.

FITTING AN IUCD

Prior to fitting an IUCD always check for the contraindications shown in Table 5.7.

Counselling points for potential IUCD users

IUCDs work by preventing implantation and inhibiting sperm transport.

IUCDs have a failure rate of 0.5–1.0% (i.e. one out of each 100 woman years).

IUCDs are effective immediately and easily reversible.

There may be an increase in menstrual loss and pain.

There is a small relative risk of ectopic pregnancy.

There is a small risk of expulsion – patient must see GP/FP clinic if suspected.

Choice of device

The addition of copper means that size can be reduced, and hence less bleeding and pain. Inert devices do not need changing.

When to fit

- Pregnancy must be excluded.
- Avoid days 1–4 of the menstrual cycle as uterine activity will increase the risk of expulsion.
- If the patient is postpartum, fit at six weeks.

Fitting an IUCD

- If previous change has been painful give mefenamic acid 500 mg orally.
- Perform a vaginal examination to establish whether uterus is ante- or retroverted.
- Using the no-touch technique and a sterile Cusco's speculum and gloves, insert the speculum and visualise the cervix which should then be swabbed with antiseptic.

- Pass the uterine sound gently through the cervical os to measure uterine cavity length; if > 14 cm, do not continue. (Bear in mind whether uterus is ante- or retroverted.) If perforation is suspected, admit the patient in order to exclude haemorrhage, and give antibiotic cover to prevent ascending infection.
- Set the 'Stop' on the IUCD applicator to the same length as the uterine cavity.
- Gently insert the IUCD, within the applicator, until the 'Stop' is touching the cervix. Ensure that the introducer (if present) is also within the applicator immediately posterior to the IUCD.
- Whilst holding the IUCD in position, withdraw the applicator and then the introducer.
- Cut the IUCD threads to leave 3 cm showing.

In the event of a vasovagal attack:

- If conscious; elevate legs, establish venous access. If bradycardia persists give atropine 0.6 mg IV.
- If unconscious; establish airway and give atropine 0.6 mg IV and monitor pulse and BP.
- If cardiac arrest occurs follow usual procedure. Always make sure that facilities for resuscitation are on hand when fitting an IUCD.

REMOVING AN IUCD

Reasons for removal of an IUCD are shown in Table 6.1.

When to remove an IUCD

Either during a period, or after seven days' abstinence from sexual intercourse, as a previously formed blastocyst may implant.

Table 6.1	Reasons for removal of an IUCD
Inert	**Copper devices**
One year post-menopause	As recommended by manufacturer – usually three years
For a planned pregnancy	Reasons as for inert devices
Because of side-effects	

How to remove an IUCD

- Aseptic technique.
- Pass a Cusco's speculum, visualise and swab the cervix.
- Grasp the threads with sponge-holding forceps or long Spencer Wells forceps and pull gently and smoothly. Excessive force may cause avulsion of the threads or, if the device is embedded in the uterine wall, damage to the uterus; therefore if the IUCD is unyielding remove under general anaesthetic when hysteroscopic visualisation is more appropriate.

Managing lost IUCD threads

- Exclude pregnancy.
- Insert long-handled Spencer-Wells forceps into endocervical canal and if threads are located remove IUCD.
- Thread retrievers, e.g. Emmet retrievers, may be tried next, ideally with mefenamic acid 500 mg, given one hour beforehand.
- Arrange an ultrasound scan (USS) if the device is still not located; an empty uterine cavity indicates a need for abdominal X-ray. Nothing seen on USS or abdominal X-ray (AXR) means that the IUCD has been expelled. If the device is seen intra-abdominally, arrange admission for removal by laparoscopy.

INSERTING HORMONE IMPLANTS

Insertion of a hormone implant is an outpatient procedure which is performed under aseptic conditions. Most implants are inserted into the subcutaneous tissues of the lower abdomen. The patient is placed in the supine position, with the lower half of the abdomen exposed. The skin over either lower quadrant is cleaned with an antiseptic solution such as chlorhexidine or povidone. Using a 5 ml syringe, containing 2% lignocaine, and a green needle, raise a bleb of local anaesthetic subcutaneously 5 cm above the mid-point of the inguinal ligament. Continue the infiltration in the subcutaneous fat of the anterior abdominal wall in a line laterally for 3–5cm. Then make a 0.5 cm skin incision along Langers lines over the skin bleb using a scalpel and push the trocar and introducer under the skin into the subcutaneous fat along the anaesthetised tract for a distance of 5 cm. Remove the trocar and, using sterile forceps, insert the hormone pellet into the introducer and push the pellet to the end of the introducer with the blunt-ended trocar. Gently remove the trocar and introducer from the incision and appose the skin edges using one or two steristrips and cover with a plaster.

ABDOMINAL PARACENTESIS

The woman should be supine on the bed and percussion should be used to localise the fluid level and exclude any masses which may interfere with the paracentesis. A sub-umbilical midline point below the fluid level is then marked with an indelible marker and the abdomen is cleaned with antiseptic. The remainder of the procedure is performed using an aseptic technique.

The anterior abdominal wall is infiltrated with 1% lignocaine over the marked area, and a 3 mm skin incision is made using a scalpel. The trocar and cannula are gently inserted, at 90° to the anterior abdominal wall, into the peritoneal cavity and the trocar is withdrawn. The cannula is then secured to the skin

125

using adhesive tape or two sutures, depending on the type of cannula being used, and the drainage tube is attached from the collection bag to the cannula. Instructions must then be given to the nursing staff that no more than 2 l of ascites is drained off in any 24-hour period.

Ultrasound examination is useful prior to paracentesis to define 'safe areas'. This is particularly true if there have been several previous procedures and the ascites may be loculated or if there have been several abdominal operations.

Any woman undergoing paracentesis should have daily urea and electrolytes (U&Es) checked and serum protein levels should be monitored every 2–3 days.

MINOR INPATIENT PROCEDURES

DIAGNOSTIC CURETTAGE

Whilst this may initially seem to be a simple and safe procedure and is not infrequently delegated to a junior member of the team, it is important to perform this operation carefully in order that the maximum amount of diagnostic information is obtained. One should only contemplate performing these procedures in an unsupervised role once thoroughly trained and confident.

It is still a common procedure although latterly more women are being assessed as outpatients using an endometrial sampling device.

- The patient is anaesthetised and placed in the lithotomy position.
- A bimanual examination is performed in order to assess the size, position and mobility of the uterus, and to check for the presence of adnexal masses.
- A Simm's speculum is inserted into the vagina, the vault and cervix are examined for evidence of pathology, and the anterior lip of the cervix is grasped with a volsellum.

■ A uterine sound is then gently inserted through the cervical os up to the level of the fundus (if retroversion is suspected, the sound will normally pass in a posterior curve, if anteverted the sound will curve anteriorly), and then withdrawn. The length of the uterine cavity is noted from the uterine sound.

■ The cervix is dilated by gently inserting Hegar's dilators, starting at 2 mm size, through the external cervical os to just beyond the internal os (usually 25–35 mm). The cervix is dilated to 8 mm.

■ Polyp forceps are inserted into the uterine cavity to the level of the fundus, opened and rotated through 90° before being closed and gently withdrawn. Any material obtained in this way is sent for histological examination.

■ A sharp curette is then gently inserted up to the uterine fundus and withdrawn slowly, simultaneously curetting the anterior uterine wall with a moderate amount of pressure. This is repeated seven or eight times, with the curette slightly rotated each time until all of the uterine cavity has been curetted. The volsellum is then removed and there should be no significant blood loss. All samples are sent for histological examination.

EVACUATION OF THE UTERUS

■ The patient is anaesthetised and placed in the lithotomy position.

■ A bimanual examination is performed to assess the size and position of the uterus

■ 10 units of Syntocinon® are administered intravenously.

■ A Simm's speculum is inserted and the anterior lip of the cervix is grasped using a volsellum. If the miscarriage is incomplete, the cervix is dilated using Hegar's dilators up to size 8 and polyp forceps are gently inserted into the uterine cavity. They are then opened, rotated through 90°, closed, and gently withdrawn. This is followed by gentle curettage, using the largest curette possible in the manner described in 'Diagnostic curettage' above.

■ If the miscarriage is 'missed' and the sac is complete, the cervix is dilated up to Hegar 10 and a plastic suction curette is gently inserted up to the fundus. The pressure is then switched on and the curette is gently moved backwards and forwards, taking care not to perforate the uterine fundus, simultaneously rotating the curette through 360°. The pressure is switched off before removing the curette and polyp forceps are then reinserted and any products of conception are removed, as described above. The whole procedure is repeated until the uterus is empty.

■ Finally, the uterus should be well contracted with no significant blood loss from the cervical os. All of the specimen obtained should be sent for histological examination.

DRAINAGE OF BARTHOLIN'S CYSTS OR ABSCESSES: MARSUPIALISATION

■ The patient is anaesthetised and placed in the lithotomy position.

■ The vulva and vagina are cleaned with an antiseptic solution (e.g. chlorhexidine),

■ A bimanual examination is performed and the vaginal vault is examined.

■ The abscess is identified and an elliptical incision is made through the vaginal skin over the surface of the abscess, along the long axis of the labia majora.

■ This skin is completely excised and a microbiological swab of the exudate is sent for culture and sensitivity.

■ The abscess is then milked to remove as much of the exudate as possible and the abscess cavity is explored digitally, breaking down any loculations present.

■ The internal edge of the cavity wall is then sutured, using interrupted 2/0 chromic catgut, to the surrounding skin, thus saucerising the opening to the abscess cavity.

- A proflavine-soaked gauze swab is then used to pack the cavity; this should be removed the following day, when the patient can usually be discharged.
- No follow-up is usually necessary, although antibiotic therapy may be indicated, depending upon the results of the microbiological swab.

7 *Follow-up of cancer*

All patients should ideally be seen by either the consultant or a senior registrar (or equivalent). It is, however, an important part of training to see such patients. The guidelines detailed are empirical. At no time has it ever been demonstrated that our current approaches to follow-up of treated cancer patients are either beneficial or harmful in terms of improved outcome. These patients require a great deal of positive support.

The objectives of the cancer follow-up visit

To determine if the previous intervention, i.e. surgery, radiotherapy, chemotherapy has not resulted in protracted side-effects or toxicity

To determine whether or not there is evidence of active disease

To reassure and inform women and their families of their current status

To plan and direct further treatment as indicated

To instigate further investigations, if appropriate

To ascertain risk, if any, to family members and if appropriate offer screening

---

Documentation should be complete and should include:

- A statement regarding disease status, i.e. well with no evidence of disease, well with evidence of disease or suspicion of disease
- Any investigation performed should be documented

- Information given to patients and relatives should be documented
- When the next visit is scheduled and, if not according to protocol, the reason for the differing interval

CERVICAL NEOPLASMS

Carcinoma of the cervix (high risk)

These cases include:

- All cases initially presenting with greater than Stage Ib
- Stage Ib cases with initial tumour diameters in excess of 4 cm
- Stage Ib cases found to have positive pelvic and/or para-aortic lymph nodes at radical surgery
- Stage Ib cases found to have inadequate resection margins at primary radical surgery (less than 5 mm clearance on any margin)

Follow-up procedures

- History with particular regard to PV loss, bowel or bladder disturbance, back pain or pain radiating to either groin or lower limb. Development of any sexual difficulties if appropriate
- Abdominal examination
- Examination of supraclavicular lymph nodes
- Speculum examination
- Bimanual pelvic examination and combined rectal and vaginal examination
- Examination of lower limbs for oedema or evidence of obstructed venous return

Frequency of visits

- Seen every three months for the first year, every six months for the second year and then annually thereafter until five completed years of disease-free follow-up

- Discharge to general practitioner with instructions for annual follow-up to ten years

Carcinoma of the cervix (low risk)

For all remaining cases of carcinoma of the cervix, the same procedures as for high-risk cases should be followed.

Frequency of visits

- Seen every three months for the first year, every six months for the second year and then one further annual visit.
- Discharge to general practitioner with instructions for annual follow-up to ten years.

Carcinoma of the cervix (Stage Ia1 and Stage Ia2)

Treated by hysterectomy

Vault smears are probably of value in this group of patients because of the frequent association of intraepithelial neoplasia that may in fact have involved more of the cervix than the invasive process. If there is evidence of complete excision at hysterectomy, vault smears should be taken at six and 18 months following treatment. The woman can then be discharged to her GP with instructions to perform annual vault smears up to five years following treatment. Should all smears be negative the patient can be discharged at that point.

Treated by local excision

If there is evidence of complete excision smears should be taken at six and 18 months following treatment and annually thereafter for five years. The woman can then be discharged to her GP.

If excision was deemed incomplete, a further excisional procedure should be performed.

Cervical intraepithelial neoplasia

Treated by hysterectomy

If completely excised, vault smears should be taken six and 18 months following treatment and a further vault smear a year later. If all three are negative, no further follow-up is required. If excision is uncertain or incomplete, colposcopy and cytology should be performed at six and 12 months with annual cytology to complete five years of normal follow-up. If all follow-up investigations remain normal the patient can be discharged at that point.

Treated by local excision/ablation

Smear and colposcopy at six months with annual cytology thereafter (by GP) until five completed years of follow-up. Thereafter patients should be returned to three-yearly recall.

VULVAL NEOPLASMS

Squamous cancer of the vulva

Women treated for vulval cancer should be seen on a three monthly basis for the first year of follow-up, six-monthly for the second year of follow-up and annually thereafter to complete five years of follow-up. At this point, should there be no evidence of recurrent disease or excessive morbidity associated with surgery, they can be discharged back to their general practitioners with instructions for annual review. These women are at increased risk of developing second neoplasms both within and outside the genital tract.

Annual cervical cytology should be performed for the first three years following diagnosis and then three yearly thereafter until the age of 65. If the woman is over the age of 65 at the time of diagnosis a baseline lower genital tract screen should be performed to include cytology and colposcopy. Should both be negative, no further cervical smears or colposcopic assessments will be required.

Specific attention should be paid to the following at follow-up visits, these should be clearly documented:

- Presence or absence of any local recurrence
- Presence or absence of any associated vulval skin anomalies, i.e. *lichen sclerosus*
- Presence or absence of any groin recurrence
- Presence or absence of lymphocysts
- Presence or absence of any pelvic masses
- Presence or absence of lower limb oedema, venous thrombosis
- Enquiry into urinary function and bowel function
- If appropriate, enquiry into sexual function

Examination with a speculum may not be possible, particularly if there is any degree of introital stenosis. In this situation a single-digit bimanual examination should be performed.

Melanoma of the vulva

Follow-up in these situations is as for squamous cancer of the vulva with the addition of an annual chest X-ray and ultrasound scan of the liver.

Verrucous carcinoma and basal cell carcinomas

Whilst uncommon, these cancers are far less likely to have metastasised locally and widely. Follow-up in these situations is therefore less rigorous. If there is no evidence of local recurrence at 24 months, these patients can be discharged to their general practitioners to complete annual follow-up to five years.

OVARIAN CARCINOMA

Non-borderline epithelial tumours

There is a high risk of recurrence in all but early stage disease. The majority of relapses will occur within 24 months. Patients should be seen six weeks post-operatively, regularly during chemotherapy when they will have tumour markers (CA 125), haematological and biochemical indices assessed. They may also have regular imaging (CT and USS) performed to determine response or lack of it.

Women clinically disease free at the completion of treatment should be seen every three months for two years, then every six months to five years and then annually to ten years. The following should be performed at each visit:

- History with regard to gastro-intestinal disturbance, weight gain or loss or change in appetite
- Any vaginal loss
- Any change in bladder function
- Abdominal examination
- Pelvic examination (combined vaginal and rectal) and speculum examination
- Examination of supraclavicular nodes
- Chest examination
- Breast examination
- Blood for serum CA 125

Any suspicion of recurrence should prompt appropriate further investigations aimed at confirming or refuting the clinical suspicion. There is no place for vaginal vault smears in the follow-up of ovarian cancer patients.

Borderline epithelial tumours

These tumours have a low recurrence rate and the follow-up is both less rigorous and less frequent. After the initial post-operative review they should be seen every three months for the first year, six months for the second year and annually to five years. The history, examination and investigations are as for non-borderline epithelial tumours.

Germ cell tumours

These tend to occur in young women and their treatment should be in referral centres. Nowadays primary treatment can spare their fertility. The risk of relapse is ever present even in those achieving complete remission. The follow-up protocol should be as for non-borderline epithelial tumours with the addition of regular serum alpha-fetoprotein (endodermal sinus tumours) or HCG for choriocarcinomas.

Granulosa cell tumours

These are gonadal stromal tumours (also include Sertoli-Leydig tumours, Hilus cell tumours etc.). They can produce either oestrogens and/or androgens. Whilst less common than epithelial tumours and generally presenting at an earlier stage, they also have a significant relapse rate and should be followed up as for non-borderline epithelial tumours.

ENDOMETRIAL CARCINOMA

Low-risk cases

Low risk is defined as Stage I disease that has penetrated less than the inner half of the myometrium and is well differentiated. The risk of relapse in these women is low. They should be followed three monthly for the first year, six monthly for the second year and annually to five years at which point they can be discharged to their general practitioners with instructions for annual follow-up to ten years.

Endometrial cancer can recur locally and at distant sites (lung and bone). Follow-up should pay attention to the following areas:

- Any history of vaginal bleeding, disturbed bladder or bowel function
- Any history of cough or shortness of breath
- Abdominal examination (particularly pelvic masses and hepatomegaly)
- Pelvic examination to include speculum examination of the vaginal vault, combined rectal and vaginal examination

137

- Examination of supraclavicular lymph nodes
- Annual chest X-ray
- Breast examination (increased risk of breast cancer)

High-risk cases

In all cases except those covered by low risk, a more vigilant follow-up policy is justified because of the increased relapse rate.

Patients should be seen three monthly for the first two years (most relapses occur in the first two years) and six monthly till five years, then annually till ten years, at which point they may be discharged back to their general practitioners.

The vaginal vault is a favoured site of relapse in this neoplasm and should therefore be carefully inspected. There are no data supporting the use of vaginal vault smears in that this practice has not been shown to improve survival through earlier detection of vault recurrence. Any suspicious lesion at the vault should be biopsied.

A proportion of women will have received vault radiation as part of their treatment. This can make vault cytology difficult to interpret.

HRT AFTER A DIAGNOSIS OF CANCER

The role of HRT in endometrial cancer is problematic and it should be avoided if at all possible. In low-risk cases, who are young with debilitating symptoms, it might be justifiable although the potential for encouraging growth in oestrogen-sensitive residual cancer cells is very real. There are always going to be situations where the quality of life on HRT justifies the potential hazard.

As yet there are no data to suggest that hormone replacement therapy increases the risk of relapse in women who have been diagnosed as having cervical, ovarian or vulval cancer.

8 Imaging in gynaecology

Before discussing the various imaging procedures available, it is important to remember that they are used in conjunction with and not to replace a **proper pelvic examination**.

Types of imaging
- Ultrasound
- Conventional radiology
- MRI
- CT scan

ULTRASOUND

The introduction of ultrasound into clinical practice has revolutionised the management of both obstetric and gynaecological patients. It is a non-invasive technique with low costs.

Ultrasound, as its name describes, consists of ultra-high-frequency sound waves which are generated from crystals that can demonstrate the piezoelectric effect. When the crystals receive the electrical impulses, they expand, causing them to vibrate and in turn they transmit compression waves into the tissues being examined. Also these crystals can receive sound waves which are converted into electronic signals and can be represented as a picture on a screen.

The frequency of ultrasound probes used in gynaecology varies from 3.5 mHz to 7.5 mHz (1 mHz = 1,000,000 cycles/second).

Patients can be examined either abdominally or transvaginally using specially designed probes. Transvaginal scanning has been available for many years but apart from its use in infertility units it has not been used in general gynaecology to any great degree until recently.

Disadvantages of abdominal ultrasound
Full bladder required
Probe some distance away from pelvic structures
Picture resolution diminished

Advantages of transvaginal ultrasound
Empty bladder
Probe closer to pelvic structures
High frequency transducers produce better images
Improves diagnosis
Useful for diagnostic procedures, e.g. aspiration from pouch of Douglas, cysts, etc.
Oocyte collection for IVF

Disadvantages of transvaginal ultrasound
Patient acceptance
Staff training

Uses of transvaginal scanning in gynaecology

Early pregnancy
Useful for validation and assessment of early pregnancy. FH can be detected at six weeks' gestation. Gestational sac can be seen as early as five weeks' gestation.

Ectopic pregnancy

Ectopic pregnancies can be excluded if an intrauterine gestational sac is seen. Occasionally an ectopic pregnancy can be visualised in either the fallopian tube or in the pouch of Douglas (extra-uterine). Despite its advantages, ultrasound cannot be regarded as the ultimate diagnostic test for ectopic gestation.

Pelvic masses

Investigation and diagnosis of pelvic masses, e.g. ovarian cysts, uterine fibroids, etc. (Large ovarian and uterine masses which are palpable abdominally are visualised better with abdominal ultrasound.)

Diagnosis of hydatidiform mole

Infertility

Monitoring of follicular growth in natural or treatment cycles

- Follicular aspiration – IVF
- PCO diagnosis
- LUF syndrome (luteinised unruptured follicle)

Oncology

- Assessment of patients with postmenopausal bleeding
- Ovarian cyst/cancer evaluation
- Bladder cancer screening
- Cancer screening in high-risk groups

Pelvic pain

May be of benefit, e.g. diagnosis of endometriotic ovarian cysts

Tubal masses

For example, hydrosalpinx occasionally can be seen.

Location of IUCD

Urogynaecology

Dynamic imaging of bladder neck in pre- and post-operative assessment of patients with stress incontinence.

Transvaginal scanning is useful in emergency gynaecology as it provides a useful tool to aid in rapid diagnosis and as patients do not require a full bladder they can remain starved for theatre if required.

MAGNETIC RESONANCE IMAGING

Magnetic resonance imaging is another non-invasive technique which uses radio frequency radiation to penetrate tissue and produce clear anatomical images. The images produced for each pelvic structure are quite characteristic, e.g. fat, bowel, gas, urine, ascites, and therefore any variation from normal is easily detectable, e.g. uterus in sagittal view has a trilaminar appearance. The appearance can alter at different stages of the menstrual cycle and certainly the trilaminar appearance can even disappear in patients taking the oral contraceptive pill or who may be postmenopausal.

The demarcation between normal tissue and tumour is quite clear and therefore it is possible to measure quite accurately tumour size and volume. MRI screening, however, is of little value in visualising peritoneal surface tumours although it is probably better than CT screening in the assessment of small volume disease.

Uses of MRI in gynaecology

Pelvic anatomy
- Very useful in diagnosis of congenital uterine abnormalities
- Uterine fibroids ⎤
- Ovarian cysts ⎬ (ultrasound still should be first-line investigation)
- Endometriosis ⎦

Gynaecological cancer
Cervical cancer – probably one of the best ways of imaging this disease because MRI can assess:

- Tumour size/volume
- Parametrial spread
- Spread into vagina
- Lymph-node metastases
- Useful also in assessing patients with recurrence of cervical cancer after previous surgery.

Ovarian cancer – not used in initial diagnosis but often used for assessment of recurrent disease. CT scanning remains the most common technique of ovarian cancer assessment.

Endometrial cancer – not usually used for diagnosis of endometrial cancer. Difficulty in diagnosis of early stages of disease. Can be useful when tumours are large with metastases to lymph nodes.

COMPUTED TOMOGRAPHY SCANNING (CT SCAN)

This form of scanning is also of value in assessing the size and volume of tumours. In particular, it has been used to measure the size of metastases in the brain and liver, etc. Unfortunately, however, it also has limitations when assessing peritoneal metastatic deposits. CT scanning has a limited role in detecting small-volume disease and is of no real value in assessing response to treatment except probably the post-treatment response in para-aortic and iliac lymph nodes.

It is generally thought, however, that a negative CT scan cannot be taken as a reliable indicator that a patient is in complete remission.

CT scanning is of limited value in endometrial cancer and cannot differentiate between Stage I and Stage II disease.

The main use of CT scanning is in establishing a diagnosis and assessing the extent of disease in patients with ovarian cancer. It is also used in the investigation/work up of patients with gestational trophoblastic disease.

RADIOLOGY

Oncology

- *Radiology* has been used in the past for assessment of metastases in patients with gynaecological cancer, e.g. lung. This method has now been surpassed, however, by CT and MRI scanning.
- *Lymphography* – In endometrial cancer lymph-node involvement is quite common and if present portrays an adverse prognosis. Pre-operative lymphography has been used to identify such patients in the past. The technique of lymphography is not easy and the result needs expert inter-pretation. In general it is not now recommended as a routine investigation pre-operatively.
- *Hysterography* – This technique has also been used to assess patients with endometrial cancer. There has been some concern, however, about the risks of trans-tubal/trans-peritoneal spread of the disease. Like lymphography, the procedure is not now routinely performed.

Infertility

Hysterosalpingography

This involves the instillation of contrast media into the uterine cavity through the cervix and then visualising the pelvis radio-logically. This technique is used to assess:

- The uterine cavity (to exclude submucous fibroids) – hysteroscopy now takes over as principal investigation to exclude this problem
- Patency of the fallopian tubes
- Uterine malformations

It is used usually as an additional test but occasionally (in the very obese patient) replaces laparoscopic assessment of the uterus and tubes.

Prior to performing the procedure pregnancy must be excluded and the investigation is usually performed after menstruation. It should not be performed if there is evidence of pelvic infection.

Complications of hysterosalpingography
- Pelvic pain – all patients should be warned that some pain and discomfort occurs at the time of the procedure
- Nausea/vomiting
- Pelvic infection

If hydrosalpinges are found at hysterosalpingography, a course of antibiotics (erythromycin and metronidazole) should be given for seven days.

9 *Routine investigations in gynaecology*

Full blood count

Important investigation not only pre-operatively but also in all emergency cases for assessment and to aid in diagnosis of patients.

Haemoglobin

Assesses whether or not the patient is anaemic and in combination with blood film can determine type of anaemia, e.g. hypochromic, microcytic – which would indicate iron deficiency.

White cell count

Useful in assessing whether any degree of infection is present. If WCC is raised, determination of type will aid in diagnosis of either viral or bacterial infection, e.g. increase in polymorphs in latter infection.

Platelets

Aids in establishing any coagulation problem. Falling platelet counts are the first indicators of impending disseminated intravascular coagulation (DIC).

Blood group

Determination of a patient's blood group is necessary as a pre-operative investigation in case there is need for blood during the operation. If it is known that the procedure will be difficult with more than average blood loss expected, then it is advisable to cross-match blood so that it is available at the time of operation. In women admitted as an emergency with bleeding in pregnancy, e.g. threatened or incomplete abortion, it is essential to group the woman because if she is rhesus −ve it will be necessary to administer anti-D to prevent rhesus isoimmunisation.

Coagulation screen

This determines prothrombin time/partial thromboplastin time and fibrinogen. Fibrin degradation products (FDPs) are no longer of proven value in any management situation except in dire cases. These are only requested if one suspects DIC.

BIOCHEMICAL INVESTIGATIONS

Urea and electrolytes

Checked occasionally pre-operatively but essential in monitoring patients with:

- Intestinal obstruction
- Paralytic ileus
- Dehydration from any cause
- Ovarian hyperstimulation syndrome (OHSS)

Liver function tests including total protein and albumin

- Monitoring of OHSS
- Suspicion of jaundice
- Screening for possible metastatic spread of gynaecological malignancy
- Severe hyperemesis

Serum alpha fetoprotein (AFP)

Screening for increased risk of spina bifida – 16–18 weeks' gestation

Raised levels found in germ cell tumours. Used as a marker – can be used to monitor response to therapy.

CA 125

(Ovarian cancer – associated antigen)

This is the most reliable marker for clinical application. It is useful in monitoring response to chemotherapy in patients with epithelial ovarian cancer. The marker has a short half-life and is useful in measuring response between cycles of chemotherapy.

Human chorionic gonadotrophin (HCG)

- Measured to diagnose pregnancy
- Diagnosis and monitoring patient's response to treatment with hydatidiform mole/choriocarcinoma
- Marker for germ-cell tumours of ovary

HORMONE INVESTIGATION

Progesterone

This is measured as an indicator of ovulation. Peak levels in mid-luteal phase (e.g. day 21 of 28-day cycle). No other indication for its measurement.

Gonadotrophins (FSH/LH)

- High level FSH/LH – occurs at the time of ovulation
- High level FSH/normal LH – menopause
- High level LH/low FSH (3:1 ratio) – PCO
- Very high LH/low FSH – pregnancy; hydatidiform mole
- Normal LH/very low FSH – exogenous or endogenous oestrogen, hypogonadotrophic hypogonadism.

Testosterone

- Occasional slightly raised levels in PCO
- Raised levels in: androgen secreting tumour – adrenal gland; arrhenoblastoma

Prolactin

Measurement necessary in patients with galactorrhoea/amenorrhoea/oligomenorrhoea.

Causes of raised serum prolactin

Pregnancy/puerperium

Pituitary tumours

- Microadenoma
- Macroadenoma
- Acromegaly
- Cushing's syndrome (adrenocorticotrophic hormone (ACTH) producing tumours)
- Brain/hypothalamus: craniopharyngioma; metastatic tumour; encephalitis; TB; sarcoidosis

Rarely in hypothyroidism/PCO

Drugs: tricyclic antidepressants; phenothiazines; oestrogen; reserpine/α–methyldopa/clonidine; cimetidine/ranitidine; metoclopramide

---

Oestradiol

Measurement of this hormone is of limited value. Its principal use is in the monitoring of ovarian response to gonadotrophin therapy in infertile patients. Occasionally it is measured in patients with primary or secondary amenorrhoea in conjunction with gonadotrophin.

Thyroid function tests

Useful as hypothyroidism and hyperthyroidism can cause menstrual problems. Small number of patients with hyperemesis gravidarum can be thyrotoxic. Rarely hypothyroidism is a cause of hyperprolactinaemia.

PREGNANCY TESTS

Confirmation of pregnancy is reliant on the detection of elevated levels of chorionic gonadotrophin (which is secreted by the placenta as early as ten days following fertilisation) and can be found in both the serum and urine of patients. It is useful to confirm a pregnancy at its early stage before confirming the viability and whether or not it is intrauterine by ultrasound scan. In the past it has been conventional to use an early morning urine specimen (tends to be concentrated) for the measurement of human chorionic gonadotrophin (HCG).

Modern pregnancy tests tend to involve immunological techniques and these give quicker results, are reliable at low concentrations of HCG and can therefore detect pregnancy at a very early stage, approximately 10–12 days after fertilisation, e.g. AuraTek® HCG which is a sol particle immunoassay and used for the qualitative determination of HCG in urine but can also be used for serum and plasma.

Another test available for urine pregnancy testing uses monoclonal antibody technology, e.g. ICON II HCG Hybritech®. This assay incorporates two different monoclonal antibodies which react with two different regions of the HCG molecule. The test carries a high degree of sensitivity and compares concentrations of HCG in the test specimen to a reference zone which is known to have a concentration of 50 mlU HCG/ml. By comparing colour changes of the test zone to the reference zone one can ascertain if the woman is pregnant and estimate the concentration of HCG present, i.e. <50 mlU HCG/ml or approximately 50 mlU HCG/ml or greater.

It is important to remember that HCG is not normally found in the urine of non-pregnant women and its presence therefore in most circumstances will indicate a pregnancy whether it be intra- or extra-uterine.

HCG can also be measured in serum by radio-immunoassay and is another method of pregnancy testing. Very low levels of HCG can be detected but this test would only be available if one had access to a biochemistry department with the appropriate materials and expertise to perform this assay.

BACTERIOLOGICAL INVESTIGATIONS

One of the most common symptoms encountered in gynaecological practice is abnormal vaginal discharge which can prove troublesome and distressing for the patient. Abnormal vaginal discharge should be thoroughly investigated as it can arise from either non-inflammatory or inflammatory conditions, or both. For the purpose of this section, the investigation of inflammatory conditions only will be discussed (see Table 9.1).

CYTOLOGY

Cytology is the study of individual cells or groups of cells. Normal and abnormal cells can be recognised. Abnormalities in nuclear morphology, e.g. nuclear chromatin pattern, size and shape of nucleus and nucleoli, etc., determine the severity and degree of abnormality within the cell.

Cytopathological techniques in gynaecology include the following:

- Cervical smear/vault smear
- Cytology of ascitic fluid
- Cytology of fluid from ovarian cyst
- Fine needle aspiration from solid neoplasm
- Peritoneal washings at time of laparotomy
- Cytology of urine – catheter specimen – at time of staging procedure for cervical cancer

The method of collection of specimens depends on the site to be examined.

Cervical smears

Cervical smears are performed using an Ayres or Aylesbury spatula (see also 'Taking a cervical smear' in Section 6). A 360°

Table 9.1	Investigation of abnormal vaginal discharge		
Condition	**Symptoms**	**Clinical findings**	**Diagnosis**
Candidiasis	Vulval itching/soreness, vaginal discharge	Watery vaginal discharge; thick curd-like cottage-cheese consistency	High vaginal swab (HVS) (Gram stain and culture); microscopy for hyphae and spores
Trichomonas vaginalis	Vulval itching, soreness and superficial dyspareunia	Thick, frothy and green-coloured malodorous vaginal discharge	Wet smears/microscopy; Gram stain/cultures
Gonorrhoea	May be asymptomatic; vaginal discharge (Complication – salpingitis)	May have cervicitis (pus exuding from cervical os); pyrexia and pelvic tenderness	Endocervical swab; urethral swab; swabs collected into charcoal Stuart transport medium
Chlamydia	Most are asymptomatic; occasional vaginal discharge; pelvic pain in more advanced tubal disease	Cervicitis; mild pyrexia; pelvic tenderness if complicated	Endocervical swabs; direct immunofluorescence technique using specific monoclonal antibodies; also enzyme-linked immunoassay (ELISA)
Gardnerella (bacterial vaginosis)	Offensive vaginal discharge (fishy odour); occasional vulval soreness, itching; worse after intercourse	Creamy white, occasionally frothy, offensive vaginal discharge	Amine test +ve; (one drop of discharge and one drop of 10% potassium hydroxide on a glass slide to emit an odour); HVS for Gardnerella vaginalis and anaerobes; Gram stain; 'clue cells' on microscopy in the absence of lactobacilli
Syphilis (now rarely seen); primary and secondary stages	Vaginal discharge	Ulcers present in genital region	Serology
Genital herpes	Pain/soreness in vulva; dysuria and retention of urine in severe cases	Painful ulcers on vulva/vagina and cervix; lymphadenopathy (groin); occasional pyrexia; secondary infection	Ulcer swabs and endocervical swabs in viral transport medium for growth of HSV

sweep of the cervical os is performed the objective being to take a sample of superficial cells from the squamocolumnar junction. The sample is then spread evenly on a named glass slide and fixed immediately in 74% OP alcohol to which polyethylene glycol (carbowax) has been added which provides a hygroscopic cover, allowing the smears to dry. Cervical smears are performed to detect cancer of the cervix at the pre-invasive stage. The cervix is easily accessible, allowing direct visualisation and in combination with colposcopy which localises abnormalities, biopsies and treatment can be performed.

Cervical smears can detect unrecognised adenocarcinoma-in-situ. This is not a specific screen or a diagnostic test but a coincidental finding.

Screening for endometrial cancer by cervical cytology is not effective in obtaining a diagnosis and other methods have to be used, e.g. histological by use of endometrial pipelle.

Ovarian cancer is often diagnosed late because it is regarded as one of the 'silent' tumours. By examining peritoneal washings and ascitic fluid a more accurate method of staging the disease can be made. A similar method can be used to follow up patients after treatment.

Fine needle aspiration (FNA)

Ultrasound is now commonly used to help in this technique, especially transvaginal ultrasound as access to the pelvic organs can be made through the pouch of Douglas. In addition to individual cells being aspirated small pieces of tissue are occasionally obtained allowing more material to be available for examination.

The material obtained can either be deposited on glass slides and a smear performed and fixed (as previously) or the material can be placed in normal saline which is then centrifuged to obtain a deposit and subsequently examined in a similar manner. In some laboratories the aspirates are collected in solution and then, with the aid of a millipore filter, the small deposits can be treated like tissue and examined histologically.

WEEKLY TIMETABLE		
	Morning	**Afternoon**
Monday		
Tuesday		
Wednesday		
Thursday		
Friday		

TELEPHONE NUMBERS

Consultant [	]	
Consultant [	]	
Consultant [	]	
Consultant [	]	
Consultant [	]	
Secretary to [	]	
Secretary to [	]	
Secretary to [	]	
Secretary to [	]	
Anaesthetist [	]	
Anaesthetist [	]	
Anaesthetist [	]	
Anaesthetic Office		
Theatres		
Outpatients		
Accident and Emergency		
Ward [	]	
Ward [	]	
Ward [	]	
Ward [	]	
Ward [	]	
Ward [	]	
Labour ward		
Antenatal clinic		
Ultrasound dept		
X-ray dept		
ECG		
Biochemistry		
Haematology		
Blood bank		
Bacteriology		
Histopathology		
Medical staffing		
Postgraduate tutor		
Library		
Other [	]	
Other [	]	
Other [	]	
Other [	]	
Other [	]	

Index